Expressionista

HOW TO EXPRESS YOUR TRUE SELF
THROUGH (AND DESPITE) FASHION

JACKIE WALKER, DOCTOR OF CLOSETOLOGY
and PAMELA DITTMER MCKUEN

ALADDIN
New York London Toronto Sydney New Delhi

 BEYOND WORDS
Hillsboro, Oregon

ALADDIN
An imprint of Simon & Schuster
Children's Publishing Division
1230 Avenue of the Americas
New York, NY 10020

BEYOND WORDS
20827 N.W. Cornell Road, Suite 500
Hillsboro, Oregon 97124-9808
503-531-8700 / 503-531-8773 fax
www.beyondword.com

First Beyond Words/Aladdin edition September 2013

For information about special discounts for bulk purchases, please contact Simon & Schuster Special Sales at 1-866-506-1949 or business@simonandschuster.com.

The Simon & Schuster Speakers Bureau can bring authors to your live event. For more information or to book an event contact the Simon & Schuster Speakers Bureau at 1-866-248-3049 or visit our website at www.simonspeakers.com.

Managing Editor: Lindsay S. Brown

Editor: Gretchen Stelter

Design: Sara E. Blum

Illustrations: Shannon Laskey

The text of this book was set in Adobe Caslon Pro

Manufactured in the United States of America 0913 FFG

10 9 8 7 6 5 4 3 2 1

Library of Congress Cataloging-in-Publication Data

Walker, Jackie.
  Expressionista : how to express your true self through (and despite) fashion / Jackie Walker, Dr. of Closetology, and Pamela Dittmer McKuen.
    pages   cm
  1. Women's clothing—Psychological aspects. 2. Fashion—Psychological aspects. 3. Women—Psychology. 4. Identity (Psychology) I. McKuen, Pamela Dittmer. II. Title.
  GT1720.W35 2013
  391.201'9—dc23
                                                        2012045491

ISBN 978-1-58270-429-6 (hc)
ISBN 978-1-58270-428-9 (pbk)
ISBN 978-1-4424-8523-5 (eBook)

Contents

Introduction:
In the Mirror

It's all about finding your own
beauty, not wishing you looked like
somebody else.

—ZOOEY DESCHANEL

Stand in front of a full-length mirror and take a long
look at yourself—up and down, from the top of your
head to the tips of your toes. What do you see?

Do you like yourself the way you are—your clothes and
your hair? What would you change if you could?

Many young girls find lots to criticize about themselves.
They want to be more of this and less of that in the misguided
belief that those changes will help them become better in
some desired way. This book doesn't want to change you at
all, but it will change the way you think about yourself. As
a result, you will find your appearance changing—and you

won't have nearly as much to criticize! In fact, you'll truly like the newer, more confident you!

If you're reading this book, you probably love clothes. We do too. Fashion is creative and expressive. It's also fun, whether you are shopping for something new, browsing magazines for trends, practicing makeup techniques, or finding different ways to wear the pieces hanging in your closet.

Throughout the book, you'll find shopping secrets from our favorite models, designers, and stylists; advice from famous fashion icons; and tips from Expressionistas just like you.

THE PROBLEM WITH CLOTHES

Clothes can also cause hurt feelings, conflicts, and even fights. And sometimes it's hard to know what to wear. You might put on a cute sundress for a birthday party only to find that everyone else is wearing jeans. You might wear a jacket that your older sister bought you in Italy when she was an exchange student, and then a classmate says it looks cheap. Or maybe you hear someone whisper behind your back that you're too fat to wear tank tops. Maybe there are girls at your school who make fun of anyone who doesn't wear—or can't afford to wear—whatever fashion item they decide is in at the moment. Maybe you've worn something you really don't like but were afraid of being excluded from the crowd or teased on Facebook or Twitter or YouTube—or even worse, if you didn't wear it.

Believe it or not, we understand. These scenarios aren't new. They've been going on for a very long time. We both remember the times our classmates made hurtful comments about how we looked. Those barbs and stings last a long time. Perhaps you can relate.

> *"People would be like, 'Why are you leaving?'*
> *and I'd say, 'Because I'm crying after you just*
> *made fun of me!'"*
>
> —BELLA THORNE

Jackie's Story: When I was nine years old, my dad bought me an expensive sweater that we really couldn't afford. He wanted me to have something special, and I was so excited! It was a pullover sweater and it had big red and tan stripes. I wore it to school the very next day. But then, during one of the breaks to change classes, a boy called me a jailbird. As you probably know, prisoners often wear uniforms with big black and white stripes. A jailbird? I felt horrible the rest of the day. When I got home, I hid the sweater in the back of my closet and never wore it again. To this day, I feel guilty about letting that silly comment bother me so much. I'm sure I hurt my dad's feelings too. He had to have noticed, but he didn't say anything.

Pamela's Story: I wore long hair and liked to experiment with new hairstyles. I was always playing around with braids and curls and clips and temporary colors. One day, I invented a style I loved: I parted my shoulder-length blond hair in the center, smoothed the sides over my ears and toward the back, and then made a low ponytail. I felt very glamorous! I couldn't wait to get to school the next day to show everyone. But when I got to my English class, a boy said, "Pam looks like a pilgrim today." I was so embarrassed to be called a pilgrim. It was a small elementary school, and everyone found out what the boy said. It turned out my beautiful new hairdo was a big, fat, ugly mistake.

POSITIVE CHANGES AHEAD

We're happy to see that some positive changes are taking place in homes, schoolyards, and sports fields across the country. We've visited elementary schools that have no-lock-out policies. That means no one can turn down anyone who wants to join a group or sit at a lunch table. Some school districts have passed no-bullying rules with strict penalties. On the shopping front, several national stores and catalogs have begun using real people instead of professional models to show their clothes. We hope more schools and retailers will do the same.

"Bullying is for losers," says Lady Gaga, who launched an antibullying campaign after a fourteen-year-old fan committed suicide because he was taunted for being gay. Gaga too was criticized and tormented for being different when she was in school.

The Bully Project, which came out of the 2011 movie *Bully*, about the painful stories of five bullied children, is another antibullying campaign. The Bully Project helps children and adults learn empathy, which means understanding how other people feel.

And then there's the It Gets Better campaign. It was founded by author and media personality Dan Savage and his partner, Terry Miller, to inspire young people who are facing harassment. Although the campaign is directed toward the lesbian, gay, bisexual, and transgendered audience, the big message that everyone deserves to be respected for who they are applies to everyone.

The Dove Campaign for Real Beauty is a project of the Dove toiletries company. The goal is to help girls and women build self-esteem and embrace their unique beauty. Dove is doing this through advertising that uses real women, not models; special events and educational workshops; and online activities and readings.

You can learn more about all these campaigns in our resources section at the end of this book.

BE PART OF THE CHANGE

We—Jackie and Pamela and our editors—want to be a part of the change by writing this book. We can't take away the mean girls and boys. We can't stop the criticism or the insults. Those are going to be with each of us for our entire lives, unfortunately. There will always be somebody who doesn't like something you do or something you wear. What this book can do is help you discover and express your true fashion personality, which we call a Fashion Persona. When you know yours and embrace it, you follow your own rules and standards in all of life. Your confidence and self-esteem soar because you know you are being the real you. It won't matter what anyone says about you. You love what you see every time you look in the mirror.

Another thing this book will do is help you improve your relationships with others, like your mom, your sisters, your friends, and your enemies. After you learn all the Fashion Personas, you will be able to match them up with everyone you know. You'll have a better understanding of how each person thinks, what's important to her, and why she looks the way she does. You might realize that the girl who sits in front of you in history class, the one who always dresses like a vampire and wears so much black makeup, isn't weird and self-absorbed. She just has a Dramatic Persona—and then you feel better about approaching her or anyone else who has a different look. You see that your mom doesn't really like your sister better—it's just that they have the same Fashion Persona. They share one small area of their lives, and there is so much more that you can share with both of them. Whatever the situation, being aware of the various Personas is a starting point for better understanding, new friendships, and greater harmony.

We'll get to all that later. First, we focus on *you*.

> EXPRESSIONISTA QUOTE:
>
> *"Looks don't matter for fitting in. It's your personality that matters."*

Getting to Know You:
A Letter to Our Readers

My mom taught me how to treat my body
with respect, to be grateful I have two
arms and two legs.

—CARLY RAE JEPSEN

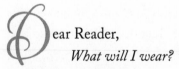ear Reader,

What will I wear?

That's the question you and millions of girls across the country ask yourselves every single morning, maybe even several times a day. Every place you go, everything you do requires making decisions about clothes. Your answer to that question is about much more than just covering your body. Clothing is a means of self-expression.

Clothing—and we're including accessories, hairstyles, and makeup in this instance; we'll break them down later—is a communicator. The minute you walk into a room, your outer appearance sends messages about the inner you. It tells the world how you feel about yourself and your life and what you want other people to think about you. When you believe you look good, you feel good. You positively glow! Everybody can see a special light in you. It's pretty awesome.

And when you don't feel good about what you're wearing, well, that shows too. Your sparkle is gone. You might even feel like the day is ruined.

EVERYONE HAS A FASHION PERSONA

We want you to feel confident, powerful, and beautiful all the time. The key is finding your fashion personality. Perhaps you call it a sense of style. We call it a Fashion Persona. What is a Fashion Persona? In simple terms, your Fashion Persona is your personal identity as it relates to and is expressed through fashion, style, and design. It is a composite of everything you love and everything that makes you feel good inside. It's the true you. Everybody has a Fashion Persona, and everybody is unique. Even identical twins can have different Fashion Personas!

EXPRESSIONISTA QUOTE:

"Don't believe beauty magazines that make you feel ugly."

The problem is that most of you don't know what your Fashion Persona is. As a result, you don't always feel good about yourself. You don't like the way you look and you don't like most of your clothes. You criticize yourself. You hate your body or your hair, and you wish you could be someone else. You keep trying different looks—preppy one week and vintage the next—but nothing feels right.

Stop! It doesn't have to be that way.

When you know your Fashion Persona, it's like knowing something very special about yourself. You know exactly who you are, style-wise. That knowledge makes clothing decisions much easier. It doesn't matter whether you are shopping for something new or if you are creating innovative combos from pieces you already own. Simply trust your Fashion Persona, and you won't go wrong. Your outer self, which is your appearance, will match your inner self, which is your Persona. You'll feel so good. You'll be happier. You'll get along better with your friends and family. We're going to help you get to this point. When you reach it, we have a special name for you: Expressionista.

> "I don't let paparazzi and gossip affect me.
> I'm here because I'm a musician, and that's where
> I put my focus."
>
> —AVRIL LAVIGNE

This book shows you how to become an Expressionista. You are about to start on a journey in self-discovery to identify your Fashion Persona and learn how to choose the clothing and all the trimmings to make you feel your most wonderful self. Don't worry—you won't need tons of money. (Moms and dads will be happy to hear that.) This practical and interactive handbook will serve for many years to come. You'll take quizzes that reveal your Fashion Persona and test your shopping know-how. You'll also find journaling exercises, assignments, and loads of advice on subjects such as buying on a budget and organizing your closet. We've included dozens of special tips, which we call Dress to Express. Keep a notebook or your computer near when you're reading this book, so you can journal what you're experiencing. Writing slows down our brains, and our thoughts become deeper and more insightful than if we just answer out loud or inside our heads. Sometimes it will be clear when you need to write— like when you're keeping score during the quizzes. At other times we'll remind you to take some time to write about what you're thinking and feeling when we prompt you to Share Your Thoughts.

By reading this book and following its steps, you'll be able to create a wardrobe of clothes and accessories that you love and feel good about wearing. Never again will you stand in front of your closet in frustration and exclaim, "I don't have a thing to wear!"

Are you ready to become an Expressionista? Turn the page.

Much love and many hugs,
Jackie Walker, *Doctor of Closetology*
Pamela Dittmer McKuen

QUIZ

Are You an Expressionista?

An Expressionista is someone who knows her personal sense of style and isn't afraid to show it, no matter what anyone else says. She doesn't need to impress anyone or follow the latest television star. She checks out the latest trends and celebrity appearances or peruses style sites online when she feels like it, but ultimately she makes up her own mind about what to wear. She believes she looks great—and she does.

Are you an Expressionista?

Find out now.

Answer the following statements *yes* if they are true or mostly true for you. Answer *no* if they are not true or mostly not true.

1. Before the big party, your friends call you to see what you plan to wear.

2. You don't mind when you can't buy something new for the big party—you'll just think up something different to do with your hair or nails.

3. It doesn't bother you when someone makes a rude remark about something you're wearing.

4. You don't have a lot of clothes, but you mostly like everything in your closet.

5. Sometimes you give your mom or older sister fashion advice, and she takes it.

6. You like to experiment with colors and combinations you haven't tried before.

7. You don't judge people by what they wear or how they look.

8. You don't buy something just because someone else does or because it's popular.

9. Sometimes you borrow something from your dad's or brother's closet to wear.

10. Clothes are fabulous, but they aren't the most important thing in your life.

Scoring: How many *yes* answers do you have? Expressionistas have lots of *yes* answers. Here's how to interpret your score:

9–10 You are well on your way to becoming an Expressionista! With this book you will learn about Fashion Personas and how they relate to your independent sense of style. You'll also be able to help your friends and sisters find theirs.

7–8 Sometimes you feel very secure in your clothing decisions, and sometimes you're just not sure. As you learn more about your personal style and find creative ways to express it, you will make Expressionista decisions all the time.

5–6 Keep trying out new looks and new ideas until you find the ones that you feel totally comfortable with. Expressionistas are adventuresome!

3–4 You're definitely influenced by other people. When you learn more about your personal style, you'll be more confident about making your own decisions. That's the first step to becoming an Expressionista.

0–2 Right now you are probably a little unsure of your fashion choices. That's okay, because we're here to help you feel more confident. Keep reading, and we'll show you how to become an Expressionista!

1

How You Look Is How You Feel:
Good Clothes Days and Bad Clothes Days

Today is another day for your inner
goddess to step out and shine.

—Jennifer Lopez

Close your eyes and think about the most wonderful day
in your life so far. Perhaps it was a birthday or a graduation or some other celebration. Perhaps you won an award or a
competition. Imagine that you are reliving that day right now.
Let your mind wander through all the sights and sounds.

**Write in your notebook or on your computer about the
occasion and how it made you feel.**

Now go back in your mind and remember how you looked that day: What did you wear? Think about your clothes, your shoes, your jewelry, your hair, possibly even your nails. How did you decide what to wear for the occasion? Was it your decision, or did someone tell you? Did you buy something new or put together a new look from pieces in your closet? Did you borrow anything from your mom, sister, or friend? Do you wish you had worn something else?

Write about what you wore and how you felt about it.

We're asking these questions for a good reason. There is a strong connection between how we look and how we feel about ourselves. When we look good, we feel good. When we feel good, the day seems brighter. We're happier. We're more agreeable. We're nicer to ourselves and to other people. People like to be around us and that makes us even happier. Isn't that what we all want?

The opposite is also true. When we don't feel great about ourselves, it's often because we don't think we look good. It's like having a Bad Hair Day, only worse. You've heard of Bad Hair Days, haven't you? It's when your hair doesn't go the way you want it to, or you don't have time to style it, or the rain makes your hair go frizzy or flat. All you can think about is how awful your hair looks.

Here's how your thinking might go: You're sure other people are looking at you, and they are thinking about how bad your hair looks. Next thing you know, you're putting yourself down even more, thinking about how stupid and ugly you are. You don't want to talk to anyone or answer questions in class because more people will look at you. And if people look at you, they will see your hair, and then they will think you are stupid and ugly too. All you want to do is run and hide.

Write something nice about your hair, so the next time you feel this way, you can remember what you love!

Bad Hair Days happen with clothes too. A Bad Clothes Day is when the leggings you want to wear are in the laundry, or you can't find your favorite T-shirt, or your sister left the house wearing *your* clogs. So you wear your mom's clogs, but you hate the color, and she doesn't have any doodads in the holes. Not cute ones, anyway.

Another Bad Clothes Day could be when you go to a sleepover and someone makes a joke about your "little-girl bunny pajamas."

Or on the first day of school, you wear a smart little sundress, and everyone else is wearing jeans. And you're so embarrassed!

Write about a Bad Clothes Day you had. What made it a Bad Clothes Day?

> EXPRESSIONISTA
> QUOTE:
>
> *"Everybody should feel beautiful. No one should feel ugly."*

It's perfectly natural to get down on yourself once in a while. Just don't do it often or stay there. Even the most secure Expressionistas have their down times, including some of the most talented and beautiful people you can think of. Lady Gaga has often said she felt like a freak when she was growing up. Taylor Swift says she felt like an outcast because she loved country music, which was unpopular in her school. And Janet Jackson of the fabulous Jackson family has talked about her brothers' painful teasing. Because of them, she believed her smile was hideous. Janet literally banged her head against the wall until she cried because she felt so unattractive. It's hard to imagine because she is so beautiful and talented.

> "I sometimes feel like a loser still.
> I have to remind myself I'm a superstar."
> —LADY GAGA

You don't ever have to have a Bad Clothes Day again. We don't want you to think negative thoughts about yourself or doubt who you are. The chapters in this book contain tips and tricks that will guide you through your entire life of shopping and wardrobe organization. You will be an Expressionista, just like Gaga and Taylor and Janet.

KNOW YOUR FASHION PERSONA

The first step to becoming an Expressionista is to identify your Fashion Persona. As we said before, you might call it your style, as in, "That's just her style to wear lots of jewelry." Or "My mom and I don't like the same things—we have different styles." But styles come in categories, as you'll see in later pages. We call the categories Fashion Personas.

Everyone has an inner self and an outer self. Your inner self is made up of all the things that people don't see. That's the part of you that knows your dreams and your fears and your most secret thoughts. Your outer self is how you show yourself to the world around you. It is made up of your appearance, your posture, your voice, and the things you talk about. People see your outer self, but only you can see your inner self. Your inner self is permanent. Your outer self can easily be changed, just by changing your clothes.

When it comes to clothing, your inner and outer selves must be in harmony with each other. When they're not, you are uncomfortable. You might think you're not wearing the "right" clothes or that you are pretending to be someone you aren't. You might even feel that no one really knows you. Here's where the Fashion Personas come in.

Your Fashion Persona is the real you. It is who you are on the inside. It is what you really like and what truly makes you happy or sad or confident or afraid. It guides you to the clothing and appearance choices that reflect who you really are. When you dress to express your Fashion Persona—and not the way some magazine or television star or classmate dictates—the inner you and outer you are in harmony. That's the way it should be. As a side benefit, you will build a wardrobe of things you love and relate to. If you are rushed to get out the door some morning, you can just grab anything and put it on, and you'll feel fine. You might be nervous about missing the bus or getting a good grade on a math test, but you won't worry about your clothes on top of it. That's the Expressionista way.

There's another benefit to knowing and expressing your Fashion Persona: you gain greater confidence when you know you are being true to yourself and no one else. Then the next time someone makes a joke about your bunny pajamas, the pajamas you love so much and that make you so happy, you can just shrug it off. After all, you're an Expressionista!

Everybody has a Fashion Persona: every girl, teen, and woman. (Men and boys have them too, but they usually don't take clothing as personally as women do. Of course, there are exceptions, but in this book, we are concentrating on us ladies!) Furthermore, all Fashion Personas are different. For the sake of simplicity, we categorize Fashion Personas into five main types. They are: Classic, Natural, Romantic, Dramatic, and Trend Tracker. And that's what we are going to talk about next.

Are you ready to learn your Fashion Persona?

Write a big YES!

2

Understanding Fashion Personas

Style is a way to say
who you are without
having to speak.

—RACHEL ZOE

A Fashion Persona is a personal identity that is expressed through outer appearance, but it's more than just which clothes you pull out of the closet in the morning. Outer appearance includes how you wear your clothes; how you accessorize your clothes; how you style your hair; and whether you wear makeup and, if so, how much. It all works together and creates a total presentation.

Your outer appearance is a powerful communicator. Everything you wear gives people information about you without actually talking to them. For example, the way you dress might say you are ready for sports. Or that you are a girly girl. Or that you definitely want to be noticed. Clothes do the talking. You want to make sure you are sending the messages you really mean to send. You do that by staying true to your Fashion Persona—after you know what it is and what it's all about.

The five main, or primary, Fashion Personas are: Classic, Natural, Romantic, Dramatic, and Trend Tracker. Every person on this planet has a Fashion Persona—you, your mom and stepmom, your cousins, your best friend, even your brother. Everyone fits into one of these categories—more or less.

Before we go farther, let's look at brief descriptions of the five Fashion Personas. We'll go into greater detail later.

The Classic Persona always looks appropriate—never too casual and never too outspoken.

The Natural Persona prefers comfortable, casual clothing without a lot of fuss.

The Romantic Persona is girly and sweet; she loves loads of small details.

The Dramatic Persona is loud and bold; she wants to stand out from the crowd.

The Trend Tracker craves brand names, designer logos, and all the latest styles.

PERSONA
SUBCATEGORIES

Some Personas have variations, or subcategories, depending on what the current style trends are and what is going on in the world. Take Geek Chic, for example, which is an ultracasual, almost intentionally antifashion look that originated with people who spend most of their time in computer labs. Think of the male characters on the hit television show *The Big Bang Theory*. Nerds, as they are sometimes called, are quite popular in some circles these days. (We love their inventions!) Their mode of dress is now a legitimate fashion style that is frequently copied. But Geek Chic is not a separate Fashion Persona. It is a variation of the Natural Persona.

By the same token, the dark and spooky Goth look is a subcategory of the Dramatic Persona. Sweet, perky Harajuku girls and many honey-voiced country-western singers are Romantics. They don't look alike one bit, but they share many of the same characteristics, such as flowing skirts, small prints, and lace trims.

But nobody fits exactly into one type. As you learn more about the various Personas and take the quizzes, you will probably find that your tastes and preferences fall into two or even three categories. That's perfectly natural. Most people lean toward one Fashion Persona most of the time, but they also favor others. You might be mostly an easy, breezy Natural for school and sports but a rocker-style Dramatic in your band. There are so many possible combinations! It's those combinations that make us all unique individuals.

Just like people are different, Fashion Personas are different. And they send out different messages. Sad to say, but it's human nature to judge people on how they look. Our interpretations aren't always correct. That's why it's important for you to identify the Fashion Persona or Personas that best make you feel like your real self. People will still judge, but at least you're doing your best to send out the right message for you.

Can you change your Fashion Persona? Well, yes. And no. It's a little like penmanship. Have you ever tried to change your style of writing or practiced a perfect signature? It's hard. If your handwriting is made up of small, curvy letters, and you put little circles instead of dots over the *i*'s, you can change it to be bigger and pointier. For a little while. Then your fingers get tired, and your hand cramps, and you go back to your regular writing style. It's difficult to write for a long time in a penmanship that isn't yours.

Occasionally, people find their Fashion Personas do naturally, without force, change a bit. If your lifestyle becomes different or you become interested in new activities, you could change your appearance and style preferences. A girl who grows up in a family with a couple of athletic siblings might, in her early years, be very comfortable doing the same things they do and wearing pretty much the same things they wear—the T-shirts, jeans, and baseball caps of a Natural. But if she channels her sports ability into competitive ice skating, she could be happy to wear the beautiful, sparkly costumes and theatrical makeup of a Romantic or Dramatic Persona. Those elements might carry over to home and school, or they

11

might not. Change in Persona is usually just a situational change—you wear different clothing for different situations. Chances are, during quiet moments at home, this girl still snuggles up in her comfy Natural clothes. They are the ones that make her feel the most like herself.

It's also important to remember that most people have one main Persona and one or two secondary Personas. So, if your life and tastes change, and you notice that you are more attracted to Classic styles than the Romantic ones you've always worn, chances are good that there is a part of you that always was Classic. Your Personas are just switching their order of importance in your life.

It can be tempting to change your personal style to be more like your friends or people you admire, but it usually doesn't work out very well. You're better off being who you really are. Here's what happened when Bryn tried to make a deliberate Fashion Persona switch.

Bryn's Story
You Can't Be
Someone Else's Persona
• •

When Bryn was in seventh grade, her two greatest pastimes were playing kickball and volunteering at her local animal shelter. She spent her after-school hours at games and practices. On Saturday mornings she walked homeless dogs to give them some exercise and attention. For her, a Natural look of jeans, graphic tees, hoodies, and other no-fuss clothes worked best. She didn't wear makeup because it wore off during all her outdoor activity, and she tied her shoulder-length hair into a ponytail to keep it off her face.

Bryn had three close friends, girls she had known since first grade. They all lived in the same neighborhood and rode the bus together. But her friends had a different style. Usually, friends like to look like their friends. Bryn's friends wore long knit tops over short skirts with leggings and boxy suede boots. They wore lip gloss and pale-blue nail polish. Their Personas were a mix of Classic and Romantic. They encouraged Bryn to dress more like they did.

One day, Bryn decided they were right, and she would copy them. Her birthday was coming up, so she asked her parents for a pair of suede boots and a couple of skirts. They agreed. Her older sister came home from college and treated Bryn to a manicure and a makeup lesson.

> **INSIDER TIP:**
>
> Learn to love resale shops (and eBay, if you're allowed to use it)—they are a great way to find bargains and an inexpensive way to experiment with new looks.

At first, Bryn was pleased with her new look. Then she was late for kickball practice three days in a row because it took too long to change into athletic clothes. When she walked the dogs, they wound their leashes around her legs and tore her leggings. A puppy got loose and ran down the street, and Bryn stumbled in her new boots when she chased it.

That did it. Bryn went back to her Natural look, the one that suited her and her lifestyle the best. She still wears the skirts, just to church and to visit her relatives now. She's comfortable again.

The bottom line: You can change your Fashion Persona for short periods of time or for special occasions. Ultimately, though, you will always go back to what makes you feel like the real you.

THE BEST FASHION PERSONA

Now that you know what the five main Fashion Personas are, which one is the best to be? We figured you'd ask that question. The answer is: no Fashion Persona is better than any other. All Personas are different. All Personas are equal. All Personas are perfect as they are—just like people, and people have different Fashion Personas.

That brings us to the two Expressionista rules of Fashion Personas. Here's the first: embrace your Fashion Persona and love her. Don't try to be someone you are not. You will not be happy if you do. You won't be smarter, prettier, or more popular. You won't be a boyfriend magnet. You won't be the Valentine's Day Princess. You will just be wearing a costume. Everything else will stay the same. If all the girls around you are rushing out to buy a certain tote bag, but your trusty back-pack works better for your Natural lifestyle, fine. Let it be. If you follow the crowd, you'll be spending precious money on something you don't need, don't like, and won't use. As one of our Expressionista friends says, "It's more important to be popular with yourself than with anyone else."

*"A ton of kids at school have made fun of me;
if I had to give advice to other girls, I would say,
'Hang loose and ignore them.'"*
—Paris Jackson

Here's the second Expressionista rule of Fashion Personas: respect the Fashion Personas of others. You should not change who you are to be accepted by anyone. At the same time, you don't want anyone to change for you. You deserve respect and so do they. We understand that friends and families often want to share the same things, but we don't have to all look alike to prove we care. We can have strong relationships with people who look totally different. It's the feelings and actions that matter.

Respect the Fashion Personas of others, and don't take them personally. It's okay if your sister takes too long in the bathroom because she's trying to get her ponytail straight; if a classmate starts wearing a red Superman cape; if the new girl wears pretty sundresses because she came from Florida, even though your Midwestern school style is more laid back.

They're okay, and you're okay. We're not the same, and we shouldn't try to be the same.

It isn't personal. It's Fashion Personas.

In the following chapters, we take a closer look at each of the Fashion Personas. Then you can take a quiz to help you find yours!

3

Meet the Five Main Fashion Personas

I don't like people to feel completely described by the clothes they wear of mine. I want them to feel that they're describing themselves.

—ISAAC MIZRAHI

Now learn just a little more of the five main Fashion Personas' basic characteristics and wardrobe favorites. Perhaps you identify with one or more—or maybe they remind you of people you know. Later, we devote an entire chapter to each persona. Then you will take a quiz to find out which one is *yours*!

CLASSIC FASHION PERSONA

A Classic is not an adventurous
dresser, nor does she want to
be. She would rather own
a few well-made garments
than several cheaper ones
that will shrink or fade or fall apart quickly.
Her wardrobe usually consists of separates, which are pants,
jeans, skirts, T-shirts and blouses, cardigan sweaters and twin
sets, vests, blazers, and jackets. Separates are versatile, because
they can be mixed and matched in endless combinations, as
opposed to dresses, which can't be changed around as much.
Most of the Classic's pieces are in solid colors, especially khaki
and navy, but she'll go for small prints, stripes, checks, and
madras and other plaids—and she loves monogrammed initials. Some Classics, but not all, like wearing soft makeup and
light fragrance. Her total look is one she knows she can count
on to be just right, no matter what she's doing.

NATURAL FASHION PERSONA

Naturals are fresh-faced beauties who prefer to show
themselves just as they are. They like their clothing to be

comfortable and easy to wear, without a lot of fuss. They usually prefer pants, often jeans or shorts, which they combine with a T-shirt, maybe a fleece hoodie, and sandals or athletic shoes. Shopping is not their favorite pastime. They tend to buy everything they need in one trip and often buy a favorite item in multiples, so they don't have to go back to the store for a while. They wear little or no makeup and rarely wear fragrance. They're fine with the clean, fresh smell of soap and water. Naturals don't want to smell like a flower garden. A little lip gloss, a sweep of mascara—maybe!—and they are ready to go. They often pull their hair into ponytails, or they wear it short. Many Naturals with hair that is wavy, kinky, or curly let it fly. "It's the real me," they say.

ROMANTIC FASHION PERSONA

A Romantic loves being a girl and all the fuss and frill that can go along with it. She likes soft, pretty clothing, especially pieces that are decorated with lace, sequins, rhinestones, ruffles, and other trimmings. She will wear separates because they

19

are popular, but she really loves dresses (especially with full skirts) and matching two-piece looks. Unlike Classics and Naturals, who prefer solids and stripes, Romantic gals adore prints, particularly soft florals and muted motifs. They lean toward pastels, especially pink, occasionally paired with black or gray for effect. Romantics like to accessorize their outfits with dainty jewelry items, hair orna-ments, and scarves. They are happy to spend time on their appear-ance: They delight in curling their hair and experimenting with new styles. They also enjoy manicures and pedicures, and sometimes try out delicate designs with nail polish—perhaps snowflakes in winter or flowers in the summer. To finish their look, they might select a floral or sugary fragrance, pale-pink lip gloss, and a hint of pink blush.

DRAMATIC FASHION PERSONA

You notice the girl with a Dramatic Fashion Persona the minute she walks into the room, and that's the way

EXPRESSIONISTA
QUOTE:

"Dream big and go for it—don't let anyone tell you otherwise."

she likes it. Her total look is what announces her arrival. Whatever the style, she does it bigger and bolder than anyone else does, and from head to toe. If ripped jeans are in fashion, hers are the most ripped. If hoop earrings are popular, hers are the biggest. She loves to layer, often mixing patterns and prints in the same outfit, and then topping it off with multiple scarves. The Dramatic adores accessories, especially large ones, because they are so visible. Accessories can also be easily interchanged to create more new looks. Dramatics love to stroll through the mall even when they don't have money to spend. They are happy to shop for inspiration—they'll study a mannequin and figure out how to copy or adapt the look with pieces they already own or can make. They are happiest when they come up with a way to wear something completely different from the rest of their classmates, perhaps making leg warmers from sweater sleeves or slipping a ruffled miniskirt over a pair of skinny jeans. As for the final touches, Dramatics may wear their hair very long or very short and sport fingernails in dark, metallic, or crackle polish. Some Dramatics would like to wear more makeup than their parents and schools allow. Until then, a sweep of mascara and berry-stained gloss—and maybe an occasional temporary tattoo—will have to do.

TREND TRACKER PERSONA

Like the Dramatic Fashion Persona, Trend Trackers also want to be noticed. But there is one huge difference: Dramatics need to be different from anyone else, but Trend Trackers need to be first to wear whatever the latest styles are. They work hard at keeping up with it all. Trend Trackers are avid readers of fashion and celebrity magazines. They bookmark internet sites and bloggers who cover fashion, and they study the clothing worn on red carpets and runways. One of their favorite leisure-time activities is shopping, where they can spend hours checking out brand names and designer logos. That doesn't mean a Trend Tracker can afford these outfits, because she can't. But she learns her lessons well and then heads out to the mall and resale shops to buy pieces that are in her budget. She works with them to copy her favorite looks. Many Trend Trackers are fearless about expressing their individuality, and they do it often. Other girls might have doubts about mixing colors, prints, and textures, but not a Trend Tracker. She's quite confident about her ability to create interesting outfits. Many people admire her sense of style and try to copy her. But by the time they catch up with her, the Trend Tracker is on to something else.

4

The Classic Fashion Persona: Traditional Values

Success to me is being happy and fulfilled, truly fulfilled, and being proud of myself and doing different things all the time.

—LEIGHTON MEESTER

Are you a Classic? Your Fashion Persona might be Classic if:

* You like to look "just right"—never too stylish or too casual.

* You are sometimes called preppy.

* You don't like your clothes to stand out.

* You prefer simple, tailored styles without a lot of decoration.

* You are not an adventurous dresser.

* You choose stripes, dots, plaids, or solids over big patterns.

* You would never wear torn jeans.

* You think dainty jewelry and small handbags are best.

* You are proud to be conservative and traditional.

* You like wearing clothes printed with the name of your school.

* You think clothes in fashion magazines are not for real people.

* You like your clothes to match (denim skirt with navy tights, for example).

* You think it's important to dress like your friends do.

* You usually wear the same jewelry all the time.

* You enjoy clubs and groups such as glee club or scouts.

EXPRESSIONISTA QUOTE:

"Being beautiful is not only how you look but also what kind of person you are."

* You would rather have one really quality sweater than three cheap ones.

A Classic wardrobe is timeless, which means it often can stretch across seasons, sometimes even years. Read the story of Cleo, a Classic who learned how to take her summer wardrobe into fall.

Cleo's Story
Classics Are Versatile
• •

Cleo and her family spent their summer vacation in Florida, where for two weeks she lived in denim and khaki shorts and an assortment of polo shirts in navy, sapphire blue, and pale yellow. She even had coordinating headbands, fabric belts, and sandals. Then it was almost time for school to start again, and Cleo stood in front of her closet and uttered those five scary words: "I have nothing to wear!"

She had a closet full of vacation clothes, but nothing she felt excited about for that first day of class. More importantly, she had enough back-to-school money for just a couple of items. While she was trying to figure out what to do, her older sister, Carolina, entered the room and offered to help. Carolina was an Expressionista. She was a Classic and knew that Cleo was too—even if Cleo didn't know it yet. "Let's go to the mall," Carolina said, and Cleo enthusiastically agreed. With Carolina leading the way, the sisters strolled through their favorite preppy boutique. Carolina selected a navy-and-yellow striped cardigan, a sapphire hoodie, a sunflower-yellow cami, and three pairs of fun socks in different blue and yellow patterns.

"That's it!" exclaimed Cleo. "I can match these with my polo shirts to make new outfits!"

Carolina replied, "That's what we Classics do."

WHAT DOES A CLASSIC LOOK LIKE?

Remember the children's fairy tale "Goldilocks and the Three Bears"? Goldilocks went into the house of the Three Bears, and no one was there. So she made herself right at home. First she tried Papa Bear's bed, but it was too hard. Then she tried Mama Bear's bed, but it was too soft. Then she found Baby Bear's bed. "This one is just right," she said. Then she went to sleep.

That's what the Classic Persona is: just right. She's not as casual as a Natural, and she doesn't stand out as much as the rest of the Fashion Personas. And that's the way she likes it. She'd rather make an impression for who she

INSIDER TIP:

If you have only one winter coat, remember that it has to go with everything. You might fall in love with a hot-pink parka, but will you be sick of it by January?

is than what she looks like. (This doesn't mean the other Personas are superficial or that Classics are always deep—they just use clothes in different ways.) Her clothes are traditional and conservative. She keeps her wardrobe up to date, but she chooses trends that will be in style for a long time instead of fads that come and go. A Classic enjoys being part of a group and often joins Girl Scouts, choirs, or book clubs.

If she's athletic, she usually goes out for group sports rather than individual ones. She is a team player.

If you are a Classic, you are in good company. She is the most common of all the Personas. The Classic Persona mostly wears separates, which are individual top and bottom pieces that she mixes and matches in endless combinations. She doesn't mind wearing some of the same things or similar things over and over. In fact, if she finds a certain T-shirt or cardigan she likes, she often buys more than one. If it works in navy, it will work in white and yellow, she figures. She is loyal to certain long-standing and traditional brand names, some of which may be favorites of her mother and even her grandmother. She is partial to small monograms—her initials on a pocket or cuff. Classics rarely adopt fads. They choose a few high-quality accessories, such as a single leather shoulder bag and one gold bangle bracelet, over several trendier, less costly ones.

The Classic style is sometimes referred to as preppy, country club, or girl next door, but the meaning is the same: traditional, conservative, and just right.

Berkley's Story
Berkley Tries to Make a Match

Seventh-grader Berkley fit the Classic Persona to a T, and she was just fine with that. She liked to wear tailored clothing, mostly in solid colors and without any froufrou. One of her favorite pieces to wear while hanging out at home was her mother's old sorority sweatshirt. She hoped to attend the same college her mom did. Maybe she'd even pledge the same sorority there.

Berkley's biggest fashion challenge was matching. She was a fanatic about it. Every day her shirt and pants or skirt had to go together. If she wore a sweater, it had to look good with the T-shirt or tank underneath. She wouldn't wear athletic shoes with a skirt. And if she couldn't find a headband in the same color as anything in her outfit, she changed clothes. Some mornings she ran late for school. "I wore my hair long today because I didn't have time to make a ponytail with no bumps," she said.

On Berkley's birthday four months ago, her aunt gave her a navy-and-tan striped cardigan. She likes it a lot but hasn't worn it yet. She has two pairs of khaki pants hanging in her closet but no navy or tan tops to wear under the sweater. She'll buy one with the baby-sitting money she will earn this weekend.

Tips

Dress to Express for Classics

* Buy bottoms—pants, shorts, and skirts—in solid colors to stretch your wardrobe. Most tops will work with them.

* Buy basic items like polo shirts and camisoles in multiples when you find a style you love.

* Set out tomorrow's clothes and accessories before you go to bed. You'll avoid the morning rush.

* Always have a clean white blouse, shirt, or T-shirt ready to wear. It goes with everything.

* If perfect matching is important to you, bring along the item to be matched when you shop or buy matching items together. Don't hope you'll find something later.

* Remember that a little mismatching is on trend right now. For example, you could pair a crew neck with thin stripes and a cardigan with wide stripes, both in the same color family.

* Don't buy on impulse or because someone else buys. You have a defined look. If you buy a pair of bright-yellow high-top sneakers, even for a few dollars at a sidewalk sale, you probably won't wear them much.

* Feel like experimenting with a little color? Start with a couple of gauzy scarves or a bright winter cap and matching mittens. If you don't feel comfortable wearing them, you haven't spent much money.

SHARE YOUR THOUGHTS

This book takes you on a journey to self-discovery. Do you think you might be a Classic? Answering the following questions in your notebook or on your computer will help you decide.

Are you a Classic? All of the time? Some of the time?

What clothing items do you own that a Classic would wear?

What clothing items would you like to buy that a Classic would wear?

Describe your five favorite mix-and-match pieces.

Name some Classics you know.

5

The Natural Fashion Persona: Unfussy and Low Maintenance

Be yourself, because everyone else is already taken.

—Selena Gomez

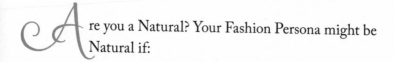re you a Natural? Your Fashion Persona might be Natural if:

* You are athletic or outdoorsy.

* Your favorite outfit is jeans and a T-shirt.

* You don't like to spend much time on your looks.

* Your clothes are mostly dark or solid colors.

* You are sometimes called a tomboy or a hippie.

* You hate wearing dresses.

* You sometimes raid your dad's or brother's closet.

* You'd rather play volleyball or soccer than go shopping.

* You won't wear something that is too tight.

* You're not in a big hurry to start shaving your legs.

* You'd rather be outdoors than in the library.

* You like peace signs better than sparkles.

* Your clothes must be comfortable and feel good on your skin.

You might have a good idea whether you are a Natural or not. But sometimes it takes trial and error before you discover the Fashion Persona that suits you best. Read the story of Bella, who experienced just that.

Bella's Story
Sports Helped Bella Find Confidence and Her Persona

Bella was a shy, quiet seventh grader, an only child who was very sad. Her mother had serious medical problems and couldn't take care of her. She never knew her father.

So Bella lived with her grandparents. Gram was a nurse at a hospital and worked long hours, but Grandpa was a retired school principal. He and Bella were home together after school. He made her a snack every day, but they didn't talk much. That was because Bella didn't talk much at all. She was sad.

One day, Grandpa bought her a tennis racket and insisted they hit some balls back and forth in the driveway. At first Bella didn't want to, but she did it just to please him, so she didn't have to talk. She found she liked the feeling of hitting the ball. It was fun, and she caught on quickly. A few days later, they went to a tennis court. Grandpa showed her how to serve and how to swing backhand. Soon she was lobbing balls over the net and making him run for them. She laughed at that. He signed her up for tennis lessons at the local recreation center. She started winning matches and then tournaments. She felt happy again, at least most of the time. Other players invited her to go out for pizza and pop, and she went.

"Sports gave me confidence," she said a few months later. "You're in the spotlight almost all the time. And when you hit the ball, everyone is looking at you."

EXPRESSIONISTA QUOTE:

"If you want to raise your self-esteem, go out for a sport and practice until you get good at it, or learn to play an instrument."

Bella's success helped her make friends on the court and at school. She also became more interested in clothes. Now she had a full wardrobe of warm-up suits, sweats, tennis dresses, and athletic shoes. Her Fashion Persona emerged as well. Which persona was she? Just what her coach said: "Bella, you're a Natural."

WHAT DOES A NATURAL LOOK LIKE?

The Natural Fashion Persona is clean and unfussy, wash-and-go. Many Naturals are athletically inclined or prefer outdoor activities to indoor ones. In fact, many of their clothing preferences originate in the sports world and become popular in the mass market. But not all Naturals love the great outdoors. Some enjoy the quiet indoor pursuits of reading or exploring the internet.

EXPRESSIONISTA
QUOTE:

"Put your heart into everything you do, not your clothes."

A Natural's typical wardrobe choices are comfortable, casual, and usually in solid colors: jeans, cargo pants, shorts, T-shirts, sweatshirts, hoodies, baseball jackets—comfy two-piece (almost always) pants dressing that takes well to the active lifestyle. Shirts are more her style, not blouses. And for the times she does need to wear a dress? Knit dresses that look like long polo shirts do just fine, or maybe a denim skirt, or a loose shift, perhaps with a T-shirt underneath. Even a tie-dyed maxi dress might do. Sometimes Naturals will raid their dad's or brother's closet: they might make belts from ties and create tunics from T-shirts and vests. As for accessories, Naturals

INSIDER TIP:

Buy three to five tops for every bottom to maximize the number of outfits you can put together.

usually don't bother. They are more inclined to tote a backpack or a gym bag than a purse. Most jewelry gets in their way. If they wear any at all, it's usually studs or tiny hoop earrings.

Naturals often don't mind having school dress codes or uniforms because it makes mornings go faster. They don't have to make clothing decisions or worry about being criticized because they chose the "wrong" things.

The Natural Fashion Persona has a couple of variations, or subcategories. We already mentioned Geek Chic in chapter 2 as a deliberately antifashion look made up of easy-fit pants, baggy sweaters, turtlenecks, T-shirts imprinted with images of fantasy heroes, and chunky shoes. Bicycle Chic and Surfer Girl are athletic variations that are identifiable by their focus on attire and gear, such as body-hugging bike shorts or swimwear and swim cover-ups designed for a particular sport. Another subcategory, Hippie, can be recognized by a primary wardrobe of jeans (sometimes bell-bottom), tie-dyed or graphic-print T-shirts, loose-fitting vests, fringed or denim hobo bags, and sandals. Although these are different looks, they all display the Natural's basic characteristics of comfortable, low-maintenance separates.

Riley's Story
Riley Gets a Buzz Cut

Eleven-year-old Riley was a Natural who didn't go in much for clothes or hair—especially hair. Riley's hair was naturally wavy, and her mom liked—no, loved it—long and flowing. It was softer than a kitten's tummy. Riley hated her hair. It kept getting tangled and twisted, and it fell into her eyes. Yuck. What Riley really wanted was a buzz cut. But she knew her mom would never agree. In fact, her mom would absolutely freak. Then Riley got an idea. In English class, she had learned how to write a persuasive speech. She got a B+ on that assignment. She knew she was able to use facts and logic, not emotion or tears or anger. That's what she did.

She wrote a paper that explained her desire for the buzz cut and outlined the reasons it would be good for her, put it in a pretty folder, and gave it to her mother. If she had a buzz cut, she wrote, she would look neater, because her hair would be easier to manage; she would have more self-confidence, because short hair suited her personality better; and she would have more time to spend on her schoolwork, because she wouldn't be spending as much time wrangling her hair. Riley's arguments were so practical even her mother had to agree with her. Riley got the haircut she wanted. Her mom kept one long lock as a souvenir and tied it with a pink satin ribbon.

Dress to Express for Naturals

* Put some variety in your wardrobe, so you don't look like you are wearing the same thing every day. Instead of buying a basic T-shirt in several solid colors, pick different styles or a style with a little decoration.

* Wear only one team or band name at a time.

* If you are concerned that you look too boyish, carry a hobo or messenger bag instead of a backpack. You'll still be able to haul a lot of stuff.

* If you don't want to spend much time on your hair, opt for a well-cut short 'do. (And get regular trims.) Even ponytails take work.

* Get a french manicure. Your nails will look neat, pretty, and natural, but chips won't show for days, or longer.

* Spruce up your wardrobe with a couple of sweaters and polo shirts. These are Classic pieces that also suit the Natural fondness for separates.

* Have fun with socks. Choose colors to match your T-shirts and polos, or small prints that show your favorite things, such as animals or sports.

* Instead of a plain, solid-colored backpack, find one in a bright hue or pattern you like.

* Find a small necklace you feel comfortable wearing all the time. Let it become your signature piece.

SHARE YOUR THOUGHTS

This book takes you on a journey to self-discovery. Do you think you might be a Natural? Answering the following questions will help you decide.

Are you a Natural? All of the time? Some of the time?

What clothing items do you own that a Natural would wear?

Which items from your dad's or brother's closet do you like to wear?

What clothing items would you like to buy that a Natural would wear?

Name some Naturals you know.

6

The Romantic Fashion Persona: Sweet and Pretty

The cutesy, sweet side of me is really fun. It definitely represents a side of my personality. But I'm multidimensional, just like every woman.

—KATY PERRY

Are you a Romantic? Your Fashion Persona might be Romantic if:

* You prefer dresses and skirts to pants.

* Your favorite colors are pastels.

* You have been called a girly girl.

* You like lace, flowers, ribbons, ruffles, and other trimmings.

* You like motifs, often involving such characters as Barbie and Hello Kitty.

* You love to get dressed up.

* You usually wear a bow or other ornament in your hair.

* You wish you were a princess.

* Your good shoes are black patent leather.

* You own a tutu and sometimes wear it just because.

* You don't mind taking time to curl your hair.

* You and your girl pals like to make or exchange friendship bracelets.

* You like to save souvenirs, birthday cards, and other keepsakes in scrapbooks or special boxes.

Many Romantics are sentimental about their clothes and their relationships with friends and family. When they outgrow their favorite pieces of clothing, they like to keep them because of the fond memories of wearing them. Read the story of Rosa, who balanced her Romantic Fashion Persona with a gift that was not her style.

Rosa's Story
Rosa Keeps the Love Alive

When Rosa's mother was a teen, she and her parents moved to the United States from Mexico. Her mother grew up, married an American, and had several children. Even though Rosa lived all her life in St. Louis, she knew her mother had many family members and childhood friends back in Mexico City. One of them was Rosa's godmother. When Rosa was six, the godmother crocheted her an oversize sweater with big red, orange, and yellow stripes, plus a matching hat, and sent them as a gift.

Rosa was a Romantic who preferred soft pastel colors and tiny designs. The sweater and hat combination were beautiful, but they didn't suit her style at all. What could she do? They were treasured possessions because they reminded her that someone in a faraway country loved her so much to make them just for her, but she couldn't bring herself to wear them. Then Rosa had an idea: she

EXPRESSIONISTA
QUOTE:

"Everyone is more beautiful wearing a smile."

45

decorated a special box to keep the sweater in, and she placed the hat on her favorite teddy bear, where she saw it every day.

WHAT DOES A ROMANTIC LOOK LIKE?

The Romantic Persona loves being a girl—and looking like one too. She enjoys spending time putting together her outfits, curling her hair, and painting her nails. She often has collections of dolls or stuffed animals. Some Romantics are interested in music or art, and some like to read books about princesses in far-off lands. Although Romantics are usually very ladylike, they can be strong and athletic. If they are into movement, they might choose dance or rhythmic gymnastics instead of rugged sports like basketball and hockey.

Many Romantic girls are sentimental. They can be found making scrapbooks or photo albums in which to preserve their special memories. And they often treasure items, like a grandmother's scarf or friendship bracelets, that remind them of certain people or occasions.

Romantics look forward to dress-up occasions. Their chosen Halloween costume is usually a

> INSIDER TIP:
>
> *Wear ruffles on top or bottom, not both. Too many ruffles make you look a bit younger than you probably want.*
>
>

princess, ballerina, figure skater, cheerleader, or feminine storybook character—definitely not a wicked witch or something spooky or unattractive. For every day, they would rather wear dresses or skirts than pants or jeans, although a frilly tunic top and crocheted shrug over lace leggings is a good casual choice. They like pastel colors, small prints, velvet and velveteen, lace, ruffles, and bows. They love accessories, big time! Romantics almost always wear an ornament in their hair, perhaps a bow or flower or small rhinestone clip. They favor small, dainty jewelry pieces like heart lockets, charm bracelets, and pearls. As for makeup, a Romantic opts for pale pink lipstick, a touch of blush, and a dab of mascara. Her manicured nails are pale and pink, perhaps with a flower decal on one hand. Don't forget the dab of sweet perfume.

The Romantic Persona has a few subcategories. One is Princess, which is characterized by extra sparkly clothing and accessories, sometimes from head to toe, and maybe even a tiara. The Vintage finds her romance in clothing of days gone by. She shops resale stores, garage sales, and Grandma's attic for her finds: gauzy print blouses and dresses, lace curtains and tablecloths she can sew into tops, sweaters that are trimmed with embroidery and ruffles, and ornate costume jewelry. The Harajuku subcategory is named for the Harajuku fashion district of Tokyo, Japan, and is recognized by sweet, little-girl layered outfits with full skirts, loads of lace and ruffled trimmings, cute cartoon motifs, and pigtail hairstyles. A fourth subcategory is Bohemian, which is a gypsy-like look with colorful floral or geometric fabrics, flowing skirts and long dresses, peasant blouses, and big jewelry.

It's important for you to know that different family members can have different Personas. Read the story of Zoey and Mia, identical twins who didn't know their fashion styles were not alike until they had a chance to choose their own clothing. Because she and her sister always dressed alike, and participated in many of the same activities, Zoey never imagined she was a Romantic until she was on her own for a short time. Perhaps you'll begin to see differences in your own household.

Zoey and Mia
Twins with Different Fashion Personas

• •

Identical twins Zoey and Mia were dressed alike since they were born. Their mother and grand-mothers selected their clothes, mostly sweet pastel pieces adorned with lace, ruffles, bows, appliqués, and other girly frills. The sisters had similar personalities, but Zoey loved getting dressed and showing off her out-fits. Mia was less interested in clothes. For their tenth birthday treat, their mom took them to a department store and said they could each have a new outfit—the first they had ever picked all by themselves. Zoey and Mia were thrilled. This was a big-time adventure!

The girls went their separate ways and zipped through the racks and shelves. When they met up in the dressing room thirty minutes later, everyone was surprised. Their mother had figured the girls would choose the same things. But they didn't! Zoey had grabbed a turquoise tiered lace skirt with matching scarf, a white T-shirt with a sequined rabbit graphic, and textured turquoise tights. She was a Romantic.

Mia's choice was quite different: a navy-and-forest-green plaid skirt, two matching polo shirts (with a little horse logo), and a navy cardigan. Mia was a Classic. Mom hadn't realized that her two daughters had such different fashion personalities. Zoey's Romantic style was similar to their mom's, while Mia's Classic style was closer to their dad's. From then on, the girls began to have separate wardrobes.

Tips
Dress to Express for Romantics

* If you look super girly, people might think you are younger than you are.

* Be careful not to wear too many frilly pieces at one time. You can wear a ruffle-trimmed sweater over a blouse with a bow, but keep it simple on the bottom.

* Ask your mom to buy you a pair of pearl (or fake pearl!) stud earrings. They go with everything, from denim to dress up. You will wear them your entire life!

* If your new backpack has to last you through middle school, be sure you will still love the Hello Kitty logo or the all-over heart design on it. Sometimes a plain pink or purple is the way to go.

* Remember Pinkalicious, the girl who ate so many pink cupcakes she turned pink? If you have a lot of pink clothes in your closet, mix it up a bit. Try

other pastels (mint green or banana yellow) or brighter, related colors, like fuchsia and tangerine. If you wear the same color over and over, it looks like you always wear the same thing.

* Add a few pairs of ankle socks or knee socks in your favorite pastels. They add a touch of Romance to your jeans. Pastel-colored camisoles and T-shirts do the same thing when worn under a tailored white shirt or a rugged denim jacket.

* Go to a fabric store and find beads, appliqués, and trims to decorate sweaters, T-shirts, and pants.

* Use colorful scrunchies and other hair ornaments to give your outfits a total look.

SHARE YOUR THOUGHTS

This book takes you on a journey to self-discovery. Do you think you might be a Romantic? Answering the following questions will help you decide.

Are you a Romantic? All of the time? Some of the time?

What clothing items do you own that a Romantic would wear?

What clothing items would you like to buy that a Romantic would wear?

Name your five favorite Romantic accents, such as trims and other details.

Name some other Romantics you know.

7

The Dramatic Fashion Persona: Making a Grand Entrance

You're lucky enough to be different—
never change.

—TAYLOR SWIFT

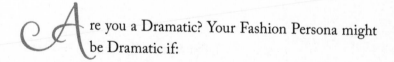re you a Dramatic? Your Fashion Persona might be Dramatic if:

* You want people to notice your clothes.

* You like big jewelry and lots of it.

* You may be described as a drama queen or show-off.

* You find vampires appealing.

* You want to streak your hair pink or blue—or you've done it.

* Your parents have said, "You're not wearing *that*!"

* You'd like to be a reality television star.

* You say, "If one bangle bracelet is good, twelve are better."

* You think clothes should make a statement.

* You never want to look like anyone else at your school.

* You love having your picture taken.

* You enjoy being on stage, especially if you have a solo part.

* You feel that the more accessories you wear, the better.

EXPRESSIONISTA
QUOTE:

"You can't be beautiful on the outside if you are ugly on the inside."

Dramatics definitely stand out from the crowd, but in some social groups or geographic locations, conservative looks are more accepted. Read the story of Lindzi, who had to move across the country, yet was able to keep her Dramatic Fashion Persona.

Lindzi's Story
Her New School Brings
a Dramatic Change

• •

Lindzi, age thirteen, was devastated when her father came home from work and announced he had earned a big promotion and the family was moving from Philadelphia to a small town in Wisconsin. And in the middle of the school year! Lindzi loved her school and was quite popular. Her classmates saw her as a fashion leader. Many of the girls loved seeing what she wore each day. She liked when they called her a drama queen.

On the first day at her new school, she wore one of her favorite outfits: a short, charcoal-gray skirt with fringe on the hem; a cream-colored turtleneck sweater; and a black faux-leather vest. She paired those pieces with black-and-cream patterned tights; slouchy black suede ankle boots; two gauzy scarves; big hoop earrings; and a chunky, black ring. But when Lindzi got to school, she faced a complete culture shock! All the girls were wearing jeans and plaid shirts, thermal vests, and athletic shoes. And they were staring at Lindzi. It was awful. Somehow she got through the first few days.

Lindzi's mom had an idea: invite some of the girls for doughnuts and hot chocolate after school one afternoon. That broke the ice. To Lindzi's surprise, the girls gave her compliments on her clothing. They shared that they might not be comfortable wearing some of the styles, but they admired her fashion sense. By the time school let out for summer, Lindzi had bought many of the same pieces her new friends were wearing, but she had adapted them to her own Fashion Persona: yellow jeans, blue jeans with rips and studs, a rhinestone-trimmed hoodie, a purple parka, and multihued running shoes. She also bought a couple of plaid shirts, but she usually wore a sequined tank top over them. Lindzi was still a drama queen, even in a conservative Midwestern town.

WHAT DOES A DRAMATIC LOOK LIKE?

The Dramatic Fashion Persona craves attention—and she makes sure to get it. She's the first person your eyes notice. That is, if your ears don't hear her loud chatter and laughter first. Dramatics do a look bigger and bolder than everyone else. If ripped jeans are in style, Dramatics' are ripped the most. If other girls are decorating their flip-flops with small jewels, the Dramatic adorns hers with big jewels, plus some feathers and beads and decals. Her lipstick is redder and her nail polish is blacker than anyone's. The Dramatic even puts her personal spin on simple things: At summer camp, when everyone is wearing black canvas basketball shoes, she chooses a red or sparkly gold pair just to stand out. If a Dramatic is athletic, she goes out for individual sports where she can shine, rather than team sports, where she has to share the spotlight. She's happy to perform a solo. Just don't stick her in the chorus.

Dramatics spend long hours shopping and planning and designing their showy outfits. Every detail must be right, and it has to be seen. Designer logos and brand names may or may not be important. A Dramatic is more interested in being seen as different and creative than as trendy. Sometimes it might seem as if a Dramatic is dressing older than her age. She is the first in her class to wear eye shadow and eyeliner to school. Her fragrance is definitely noticeable. Sometimes people look at her and say, "I could never wear *that*." But that's the very idea. A Dramatic doesn't want you to look like her. She's one of a kind.

> INSIDER TIP:
>
> It's fine to wear two or more patterns if you balance them out with a longer, plain piece. Try layering a couple of patterned tops with skinny jeans or a printed top and wildly textured leggings under a solid tunic.

Variations, or subcategories, of the Dramatic Persona include Rock Star, Goth, and Motorcycle Chic. All three subcategories incorporate a lot of head-to-toe black into their wardrobes, but there are subtle differences. Rock Star emulates the onstage look of popular musical performers, often with slim-fitting separates and highly decorated pants or jacket. A Goth look is usually entirely black and accessorized with rips, studs, chains, skulls, and other hardware. Motorcycle Chic includes real- or faux-leather jackets and pants or leggings, driving gloves, and oversize sunglasses.

It's important to note that any look can become Dramatic if it is taken to an extreme. For example, the Harajuku clothing sold in mainstream department stores is quite tame—and Romantic—compared to Gwen Stefani's Harajuku Girls backup singers, who wear contrasting light-and-dark makeup, sculpted hairdos, and highly styled accessories. Conversely, Dramatic looks can be toned down to suit other Personas. A motorcycle jacket in sapphire blue, for instance, could be worn by Dramatics, Classics, or Romantics, depending on the pieces they pair it with.

Sometimes Dramatics are misunderstood by other people, both your age and older. That's because it's common to make judgments about those who look different. They might be envious of your amazing sense of style, or they might be a little fearful if your appearance is dark. We agree that it's not fair. If you are a Dramatic who has some challenging relationships, it might take more effort on your part to make friends, like Lindzi learned at the beginning of this chapter. Here is Carson's story. Some neighborly advice guided her to happier times with her mother.

Carson's Story
Two Fashion Personas, Two Viewpoints

Carson and her mother were frequently at odds, usually about the way Carson looked. Carson was crazy about clothes, and she loved spending endless hours putting together outfits and getting dressed just so. She was especially good at making unusual color combinations and mixing contrasting prints in the same outfit. One time she and her mom went to a mall fashion show. Carson wore an emerald-green vintage sundress she found at a garage sale, the gray ruffled sweater cape she got for her birthday, and green flip-flops she decorated with big, red silk flowers she bought at a craft store. She also

FAMOUS
DRAMATICS

Lady Gaga,
Katy Perry,
Nicki Minaj,
Jessie J, Snooki,
Willow Smith,
Gwen Stefani

made a fascinator—a small headpiece—from more silk flowers and pinned it in her hair. It was the fascinator that upset her mom that time.

"You can't wear that thing out of the house!" she said.

Carson started to cry, and then her mom relented. Neither one of them spoke on the way to the shopping center. They got to the show and sat in the front row. Several people complimented Carson on her fascinator, even the fashion show commentator. Carson beamed, but she knew her mom still didn't like it. When they got home, Carson visited a neighbor, Amy, who was a costume designer for an opera house in the city. Carson always told Amy about her fights with her mother.

Amy listened and then she said, "The reason your mother doesn't understand you is you are a Dramatic and your mother is a Natural."

Carson didn't know what Amy was talking about. And then Amy explained the five main Fashion Personas. Amy had to know about Fashion Personas because she was designing clothes for various characters and performers.

That was it! That was what the disagreements were about. Mom didn't understand Carson's fashion choices because they were things she wouldn't wear herself. Carson went home, and after helping with the dinner dishes, she asked her mom if they could talk. Carson shared her new knowledge about Fashion Personas while her mother listened intently. They even looked through a clothing catalog together and identified pieces that would suit the different Personas. Then they went out for ice cream together. A few days later, Mom came to Carson's room. Mom had to go to a wedding in a few weeks and wondered if her daughter would help her figure out what to wear.

"But I'm not wearing a fascinator!" she said.

Carson just laughed, and said she'd be happy to put together an outfit that a dressed-up Natural would be pleased to wear.

Tips
Dress to Express for Dramatics

* Stick to one theme at a time. It's okay to be a little outrageous, but you will look silly if you pile on a whole bunch of totally unrelated pieces.

* Buy clothing in your size, so it doesn't overpower you. One oversize piece, like a boyfriend jacket or a huge bag, is great, but keep the rest of your pieces in scale with your figure.

* The Dramatic's subcategories are usually fads. Don't spend a lot of money on them until you have all the basics. Every girl, even a drama girl, needs a white T-shirt and a black T-shirt.

* Metallics and glitter are fun, but wear one or two at a time. Definitely do not wear glitter everything.

* Sometimes it's a little bit scary for people to be around Dramatics. If you ever feel lonely, maybe it's because you seem, well, intimidating. Remember to always be friendly and mind your manners.

* Be careful when buying presents for your family and friends. You might adore the newest crackle nail polish in black or silver, but your aunt might not have the same taste.

* Individualize your tennis shoes with an assortment of colorful shoelaces and charms.

* Before you spend your entire allowance on one great skirt or an outstanding pair of shoes, be sure you can wear it in a few different ways—and ask the sales associate when it will go on sale.

* Buttons are a great way to individualize a piece of clothing, especially when you mismatch them. Find buttons on sale at a fabric store or buy inexpensive jackets and dresses at a resale store and cut the buttons off to use someplace else.

When taken too far, a Dramatic look can seem costume-y. You want to be noticed but not presumed to be on your way to a Halloween party. Check the mirror before you leave the house or get a second opinion.

SHARE YOUR THOUGHTS

This book takes you on a journey to self-discovery. Do you think you might be a Dramatic? Answering the following questions will help you decide.

Are you a Dramatic? All of the time? Some of the time?

What clothing items do you own that a Dramatic would wear?

What clothing items would you like to buy that a Dramatic would wear?

Name five items in your wardrobe that make you stand out from the crowd.

Name some Dramatics you know.

8

The Trend Tracker Fashion Persona: Up to the Minute

Playing dress-up begins at age five and never truly ends.

—KATE SPADE

Are you a Trend Tracker? Your Fashion Persona might be Trend Tracker if:

* You would never wear the same outfit twice in one week.

* Your friends often ask you for fashion advice.

* You have been called a fashionista.

* You study fashion magazines, runways, and red carpets to see what people are wearing.

* You love being the first in your group to sport a new trend.

* You place importance on names of brands, stores, and designers.

* You have refused to wear something that was out of style.

* Your parents say you spend too much time on your clothes.

* You don't like your clothes to be too match-y.

* You're happy to spend extra time on your hair to get the look you want.

* You wore flowered pants before anyone else did.

* You love to experiment with new looks.

* You hope to be featured on the cover of a magazine.

As you may have noticed, a Trend Tracker loves clothes and spending time on her appearance. She also enjoys learning about designers and new fashions. But that doesn't mean spending lots of money on clothes and magazines. In the following story, Harper shares some of her budget-saving tips.

• •

Harper, a twelve-year-old fifth grader and a true Expressionista, experimented with different Fashion Personas. She was interested in television and movie characters, so she copied looks from *Hannah Montana* and wore an *iCarly* T-shirt. Then she was into vintage looks, with peace signs, love beads, and small floral patterns. She did a little bit of punk and goth. She thought about doing rock 'n' roll next.

"I'm not a trend follower," she said. "I make up my own outfits, and people follow me."

Did Harper have a fairy godmother or an unlimited allowance to be able to afford all these clothes? She didn't. She was creative. Her mother, a single mom on a tight budget, took her to Goodwill and other resale stores, gave her ten dollars, and let her choose the pieces she wanted.

"Goodwill is a great place to get lots of inexpensive clothes, and if you change your mind a couple of weeks later, it doesn't hurt," Harper's mom said.

Harper searched online for styles and combinations she liked, printed the photos, and figured out how the look was put together. For example, she would see someone wearing capri jeans with a gauzy printed top and a wedge sandal. She couldn't buy all those items, but she could look through her closet and Goodwill to make or add in those items piece by piece. One time she bought a pair of jeans for one dollar just to cut off the legs and make denim leg warmers.

"Harper gets her ideas mostly from television shows and YouTube, not so much from her friends, because she likes to be different," her mom said. "YouTube is like the big sister she never had."

WHAT DOES A TREND TRACKER LOOK LIKE?

The Trend Tracker Fashion Persona is passionate about clothes. She thrives on knowing what's going on in the fashion world. She spends a great deal of time reading fashion and celebrity magazines, watching fashion videos on YouTube, cruising the mall, and trying on clothes. She knows all the designers, brands, logos, and stores, and she frequently drops their names into her conversations.

EXPRESSIONISTA QUOTE:

"Don't try to be somebody else— they might be trying to be you."

A Trend Tracker is quite firm about her fashion loves and hates. What she loves most is being the first in her group to sport a new trend. She wore dangly feathered earrings and flowered jeans before anyone else. She has a collection of fascinators—those artistic head-

INSIDER TIP:

Sign up for the mailing list of your favorite stores. Many retailers send out monthly coupons or frequent-shopper discounts.

✳

pieces that are sort of a hat and sort of a hair ornament. What she hates is wearing anything out of style. She doesn't mind fads, because they are up to the minute. But she doesn't like knockoffs or imitations.

Some Trend Trackers are highly inventive. They love to create new looks by combining recent purchases with pieces they already own or with pieces they make. Or they put their own special twist into a traditional piece. For example, suppose a Trend Tracker's school basketball team is playing in the regional competition, and the coach asks everyone in the school to wear a T-shirt in school colors—blue and white—on game day. The Trend Tracker obliges, but she might accessorize the shirt with a blue-and-silver infinity scarf (the kind that makes a big loop) and a large silver hair clip. Quite often, Trend Trackers set the examples and trends for their peers. As for cosmetic touches, Trend Trackers wear makeup that works with the particular looks they want to achieve—could be none, could be a lot. They change their hairstyles, and sometimes hair color, often. Their preferred fragrances have celebrity names attached.

Trend Trackers and Dramatics may appear similar, and they both want to stand out—but there is a world of difference. Trend Trackers want everyone to know how fashion savvy they are, and their look changes frequently according to what is in and what is out. They want to show off their brand names and designer logos. A Dramatic doesn't care about that as much. Dramatics choose dark colors and strong contrasts and may wear several outstanding pieces over and over. Trend Trackers wear any color, light or dark, and any style as long as it is current fashion. Trend Trackers are like chameleons—constantly changing—whereas Dramatics are more predictably dark and bold.

> ### FAMOUS TREND TRACKERS
>
> Blake Lively,
> Brittany S. Pierce
> (character on GLEE),
> Tori Spelling,
> Kelly Osbourne,
> Rachel Bilson,
> Kim Kardashian,
> Miss Piggy

Trend Trackers have no subcategories, although they may sometimes be given nicknames: Fashionista, Trendsetter, Miss Thing, and Supermodel.

True Trend Trackers can be difficult to detect, especially among celebrities. We see them either as television and movie characters or on the red carpet—occasions when they are conveying an image. We usually don't see them in their everyday lives enough to know who they really are. You can probably figure out which classmates are Trend Trackers because you see them on a daily basis. We know

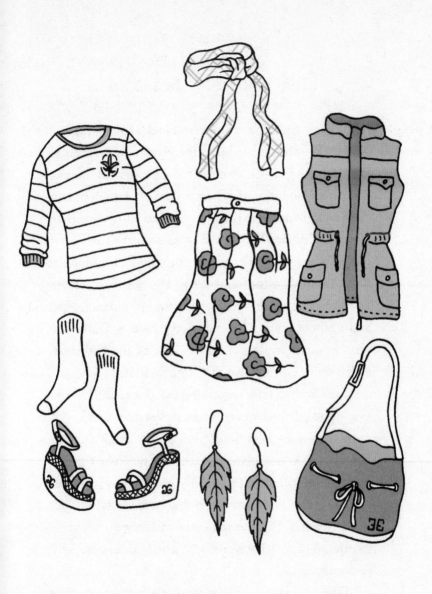

Miss Piggy is a Trend Tracker because she is the same personality on-screen and offscreen. She always wears the latest everything—and flaunts it.

Trini's Story
Trini Finds Her Own Style

. . . .

More than anything, twelve-year-old Trini wanted to be popular. She decided that the way to do that was to look like the girls who were. So she picked out three of the most glamorous girls in her class and studied their clothes, right down to their jewelry and hairstyles. Then she copied them. When one wore a short denim skirt with a long hooded sweater, textured tights, and ballet flats, Trini wore the same outfit the next day. When another girl wore flowered jeans, two layered tank tops, and a crochet shrug, Trini copied that as well. And so on. One day, while she was in one of the bathroom stalls, she overheard two of the girls talking.

"I think that Trini is stalking us," one said. "Do you ever notice that whatever we wear, she does too?"

Trini was horrified! She didn't think anyone would notice her plan, not that it was working. It wasn't. She still wasn't popular with anyone except her dog, Maxxie. Trini was too embarrassed to talk to her mom or sister. But she felt comfortable with her god-mother, Vinny, who worked at a furniture store as a senior designer.

"Girl, you don't need somebody else's style; you need your own style," Vinny told her.

The next weekend, Vinny took Trini to the mall and to a couple of resale shops. "We're just going to play," said Vinny. She wanted to see what kinds of clothes Trini liked for herself when no one else was around. It turned out that Trini had a talent for mixing different patterns and unrelated colors. When she put together a purple-and-white checked skirt, a black-and-white striped T-shirt, a cranberry cardigan, mustard-gold tights, and emerald-green ballet flats, Vinny approved, and she bought the clothes. At one of the resale shops, Trini found some old-fashioned metal keys. She decided to string them on a velvet ribbon and wear them as a necklace.

After that, Trini felt more confident about putting together her outfits. *Forget being popular. This is who I am, and if people think I look funny, too bad*, she thought. One day a teacher who admired Trini's creativity asked if she would help design and make the costumes for the school play. Trini happily agreed. She was so busy with the play that she barely noticed all the girls who were wearing old-fashioned keys around their necks. Trini had found her inner Trend Tracker.

Tips
Dress to Express for Trend Trackers

* Don't buy a new item on first impulse. Wait a couple of days to see if you still want it. Lots of times you'll change your mind. That means you can save your money for something you really love.

* Display one focal point at a time. For example, if you wear an armful of sparkly bangle bracelets, keep the rest of your jewelry simple.

* Don't buy something that doesn't go with anything you own. You'll just have to buy more things to go with it. Buy pieces that go with at least three things already in your wardrobe.

* Beware of fads. They go out of style very fast.

* Wear one designer name or logo at a time—you're not a billboard.

* Be gracious about sharing your fashion expertise with others.

* Give compliments as well as receive them.

* Take photos of your favorite outfits: they will help you remember whether you want to wear that idea again or if you don't want to repeat.

SHARE YOUR THOUGHTS

This book takes you on a journey to self-discovery. Do you think you might be a Trend Tracker? Answering the following questions will help you decide.

Are you a Trend Tracker? All of the time? Some of the time?

What clothing items do you own that a Trend Tracker would wear?

What clothing items would you like to buy that a Trend Tracker would wear?

Where do you learn about the latest fashion trends?

Name some Trend Trackers you know.

9

Who Am I?
Take the Fashion
Persona Quiz

The most important thing is to
believe you are beautiful.

—Miss Piggy

Now that we have introduced you to the five main
Fashion Personas, we know you are wondering
which one is yours so you can learn all about it. Or maybe
you have an idea or two. It's time to have some fun and find
out for sure by taking the Fashion Persona Quiz.

Here is what you do: Number a blank page in your notebook or on your computer one to ten. Read each of the
following questions. Beside each number on your page,
record the letter of the answer that you like most or that fits
you the closest. Another thing: choose answers that please

you, not ones that your family or friends would want you to pick. This is just about you. Got it?

Don't look ahead to the scoring, and don't worry if your answers seem scattered. Remember that almost everyone is a mixture of two or three Fashion Personas. Be totally honest, and enjoy the exploration.

QUIZ
The Fashion Personas— Discovering the True You

. . . .

1. Your school has a dress code or requires you to wear a uniform. How do you feel about it?
   A. A dress code makes it easier to get ready in the morning.
   B. I hate it! I need to look different from everybody else.
   C. It's okay—I can still wear my flower headbands and carry my floral-print backpack.
   D. A uniform is one of our school's traditions. That's what we do.
   E. I don't like anyone telling me what to wear—I want to set the styles.

2. Of the following style choices, what would you rather wear?
   A. A white T-shirt and denim cut-off shorts

B. My Hello Kitty sparkle T-shirt with striped leggings

C. My flowered shirt with the ruffled hem

D. A polo shirt and khakis

E. The jeweled flip-flops Mom bought me last weekend

3. You are shopping for a new pair of casual shoes. What is the first style you go for?

A. Canvas sneakers, probably navy

B. Something with a platform or wedge heel, definitely

C. Pink flip-flops with a flower trim

D. Ballet flats in blue canvas

E. I'll tell you after I check the fashion magazines.

4. Your aunt offers to take you shopping and buy you a new pair of jeans. Which style describes you best?

A. They just have to be comfortable, not too tight; stretchy fabric is the best.

B. Black, skinny, and pre-ripped

C. Lace trim or a touch of eyelet on the pockets

D. Nothing too fashion-y—maybe a simple capri

E. It's got to have a designer label!

5. What are your favorite colors to wear?

A. Dark blue

B. Either black or anything very bright

C. Pink, pink, pink! Did I mention pink?

D. Beige, navy, or white

E. Whatever's hot this season

6. What kind of jewelry suits you the best?
   A. I don't wear much jewelry, just my leather bracelet or, for religious services and dressier occasions, little earrings.
   B. Big and colorful—especially dangly earrings and chunky rings
   C. My Cinderella charm bracelet
   D. My grandmother gave me a thin, silver chain with my initial—I wear it every day.
   E. I love jewelry but only the newest styles. Sometimes I make my own.

7. How do you feel about nail polish?
   A. Yuck.
   B. I love sparkly, bright colors, like blue and green and black.
   C. I wear light pink or sometimes have a french manicure.
   D. I like only clear or very light colors.
   E. I match my polish to my outfits—sometimes I change every day.

8. Which of the following would you prefer to receive for a birthday present?
   A. A new backpack with lots of pockets

B. Sequined high-tops and patterned tights

C. A ruffled cardigan

D. A plain navy-blue hoodie

E. A subscription to a fashion or celebrity magazine

9. How do you feel about wearing makeup?

   A. Same as nail polish: yuck. Lip balm is okay.

   B. I love wearing makeup, and I'm very good at putting it on, even eyeliner.

   C. I go for pale-pink lip gloss and a touch of blush and mascara.

   D. I wear very light colors, if anything.

   E. I study the cosmetics ads and music videos to learn the latest trends.

10. Your cousin has invited you to her birthday sleepover next week. What will you wear?

   A. A plain T-shirt and sweatpants

   B. A bright, strappy nightgown and feather slippers

   C. My flannel pj's with the little hearts and my bunny slippers

   D. A tank top with long pajama pants

   E. I'll have to buy something before the party.

Scoring: Add up the number of As, Bs, Cs, Ds, and Es, and write the totals down.

Ten Fashion Mistakes to Stop Making Right Now

1. Wearing something to impress someone else

2. Mixing more than two or three Personas in one outfit

3. Wearing anything too big or too small

4. Believing you need a lot of clothes

5. Believing you must have certain pieces of clothing to fit in with a group

6. Wearing anything rumpled, dirty, or (not intentionally) torn—including your shoes

7. Not giving yourself enough time to choose your outfit and get dressed

8. Not accessorizing

9. Criticizing someone's appearance without understanding her Fashion Persona

10. Criticizing your appearance without understanding your Fashion Persona

Expressionista Assignment:

In your notebook or on your computer, name your biggest fashion mistake and list what you are going to do to stop making it.

If you have mostly As: Your Fashion Persona is Natural. You're an outdoorsy girl with an active lifestyle. Easy, low-maintenance dressing gets you out of the house quickly and keeps you on the go. Check out chapter 5 for more on your Persona.

If you have mostly Bs: Your Fashion Persona is Dramatic. You're a girl who wants to be noticed. You use clothing to showcase your creative energy and self-expression. Go to chapter 7 to see more about how you dress and how to experiment.

If you have mostly Cs: Your Fashion Persona is Romantic. You're a girly-girl and proud of it. Bring on the lace, bows, rickrack, and other frilly touches to reveal your sweetheart taste. Chapter 6 is all about how you can express yourself.

If you have mostly Ds: Your Fashion Persona is Classic. You're a traditional girl with a timeless look. A wardrobe of basics, mixed with a few modern updates, takes you anywhere. Read chapter 4 to see tips and tricks about how you like to dress.

If you have mostly Es: Your Fashion Persona is Trend Tracker. You take fashion seriously and follow the trends. When something is in style, you want to have it first. Chapter 8 is for you!

Most girls find that most answers fall into one Fashion Persona and a couple answers fall into one or two others. The Fashion Persona with the most answers is your primary Persona, and the others are your secondary Personas. If you're still not sure about which Persona or Personas are yours, ask yourself if your clothing expresses the real you, or if you are trying to be what you think other people want you to be. As you come to know yourself better and better, your primary Fashion Persona will emerge. Keep reading for further insight and inspiration.

10

Finishing Touches for Your Fashion Persona

Whipping your hair means not being
afraid to be yourself.

—WILLOW SMITH

Every outfit looks more intentional—like you planned
what to wear rather than picking just anything from
your closet—with an accessory or two. Even if you are spending an afternoon at the beach, you need something on your
feet, a pair of sunglasses, a towel, and a bag to put things in.
Some of you will add a toe ring and ankle bracelet. These are
all opportunities to show off your sense of style.

But first, what is an accessory? Your wardrobe is made up
of two parts: clothing and accessories. Clothing is the garments you wear on your body. Those are the shirts and pants
and skirts and dresses. We use them mainly to cover up.

Accessories are the small pieces like bags, shoes, jewelry, scarves, belts, hair ornaments, and sunglasses. Some accessories are functional, which means they have a purpose. Shoes, for instance, protect our feet. Belts hold up our pants and keep our shirts tucked in. Other accessories, like jewelry and scarves, are purely decorative. They can make an outfit prettier or trendier or look more polished. Many accessories do both jobs. Hats, for example, shield us from the sun and rain. They can also be quite ornate, like the hats women wear for the Kentucky Derby horse race or the fascinators many guests wore to the royal wedding of Kate Middleton and Prince William.

Decorative or functional, in today's fashion world, all accessories come in a wide assortment of styles. That's great news, because every Fashion Persona has lots of splendid choices. Just look:

CLASSIC: You love pieces that harmonize with your outfit and pull it all together. You prefer small accessories, if any, to oversize or embellished ones. A little bit of glitter or lace is fine, but not layers and layers of it. If you want to experiment beyond your usual conservative look, choose one awesome item, perhaps a slim-brim fedora hat, a checkered or polka-dotted vest, or a dangly earring. Keep the rest basic.

Try: leather cross-body minibags, shoulder bags, or saddle-bag backpacks in neutral or solid colors; headbands or barrettes; stud earrings or small hoops; multiple slim bracelets, one wide bangle, or charm bracelets; a fine necklace chain with a single pendant; low-top tennis shoes, loafers, ballet flats, kitten heels, Mary Janes, brogues, deck shoes, white or solid-colored sneakers, boxy suede boots with buttons, or rubber rain boots with matching inserts.

To be adventurous, how about a pair of ballet flats in an animal print?

NATURAL: You're an on-the-go girl who wants her fashion to be quick and easy. Your accessories should be that way too. Keep them simple, plain, and small—if at all. If you'd rather skip the earrings or save them for special occasions, that's okay.

Try: rugged-fabric backpacks or sports duffels, drawstring backpacks, mini shoulder bags or wristlets, or messenger bags; baseball caps, newsboy caps, or trapper hats; denim vests; bandanas or gauzy scarves; small necklaces or bracelets made from leather, rubber, string, tiny beads, or shells; stud or small hoop earrings; arm warmers or fingerless gloves; mismatched socks; espadrilles, moccasins, deck shoes, undecorated flip-flops, high-top basketball-style athletic shoes, cross trainers, or rubber rain boots with athletic socks.

To be adventurous, how about a faux-leather vest?

ROMANTIC: You love being a girl and all the sugar and spice that comes with it. Your clothes are sweet and pretty and youthful, and your accessories are more of the same. Look for lots of delicate detailing.

Try: handbags or totes in floral or other prints; ruffled, lace, or crocheted shrugs or vests; tutus; delicate pearl jewelry, locket necklaces, or charm bracelets; floppy straw hats; headbands, barrettes with bows or tiny rhinestones, or a scarf wrapped around your head and tied in a floppy bow; ballet flats, Mary Janes, strappy sandals, clean white sneakers,

embellished flip-flops, boxy
suede boots in sparkles or in
colors, or rubber rain boots
in a pretty pattern.

To be adventurous, how
about a cross-body handbag
with all-over studs?

DRAMATIC: You love being in the spotlight! Your
clothes are attention getters—big, bold, and bright.
Your accessories should be noticeable too—the more,
the better. And they don't have to match all the time!

Try: anything with bright sparkles or
vivid graphics or studs; oversize totes
with a message or designer or knockoff
handbags; layered scarves; chunky
rings or big beads; thin bangles in
multiples; big dangly earrings or large
hoop earrings; bold hair ornaments;
temporary tattoos; feather boas; patterned or brightly
colored tights; gladiator sandals, platform or wedge
heels, glittery boots, metallic or brightly hued boat
shoes, or high-top wedge-heel basketball shoes.

To be adventurous, make tie-dyed tights—with
parents' supervision. This can get messy.

TREND TRACKER: You study runways, red carpets, magazines, music videos, and YouTube fashion channels to find the latest trends and fads. Then you make them your own. Have fun but be careful not to pile on too many new ideas at one time. You'll end up looking a bit messy instead of like a star.

Try: lots of color; brightly hued tights, leggings, or knee socks; big, bold shopping totes; chunky metal jewelry in gold and silver tones; big brooches and rings with colorful crystal stones; collar necklaces; geometric-print scarves; cell phone covers and cases in pretty prints.

To be adventurous, wrap a long T-shirt with three thin belts in varying colors.

Here's a tip that all Personas can use to dress to express: Express yourself with a fashion signature. A signature is an item you wear every day to make yourself stand out from the crowd. It could be a heart pin or mismatched socks or a particular style of hair ornament. It could also be a fragrance. A signature makes you memorable.

Expressionistas and School Uniforms

Many schools require students to dress in a certain way while they are in class. Perhaps yours does too. Some dress codes are very strict. They require a specific skirt (and skirt length), shirt, and blazer or sweater. Other dress codes are relaxed. They might say something like students must wear a school polo shirt but with any navy, black, or tan pants. Uniforms and dress codes don't matter to an Expressionista. She knows she can still express herself, no matter what the rules say. Here are some of the possibilities:

* headbands, clips, and other hair accessories

* ponytails, pigtails, braids, updos, buns, chignons, bangs, no bangs, long bangs

* tennis shoes, flip-flops, sandals, loafers, wedges, platforms, ballet flats, jelly flats

* colored or patterned tights, mismatched socks, shoelace charms

* nail polish art

* handcrafted wallets and purses

* jewelry, especially bracelets, necklaces, and earrings—handmade or in multiples

* lanyards and backpacks decorated with pins, charms, decals, appliqués, stickers

* locker decorations, including small, battery-operated chandeliers

SHARE YOUR THOUGHTS

These questions will help you explore your feelings about your school's dress code or uniform, and inspire you to let your sense of style shine through. If your school does not have a dress code, you can skip this section. Or think about other parts of your life that have an informal dress code—for example, you're expected to wear a certain style for religious services or when you visit your relatives. Adjust the questions below to get you thinking about those times: How do you feel about those expectations? Does your older sister, for example, keep her own style while still following the rules?

What is the dress code at your school?

How do you feel about your school's dress code?

How do some of your classmates personalize their uniforms?

Name five ways you can personalize your school uniform.

11

What If I Have More than One Fashion Persona? (Hint: You Probably Do.)

I know not everyone will like me, but this is who I am, so if you don't like it, tough.

—BRITNEY SPEARS

After taking the Fashion Persona Quiz, you may have found that not all your answers match up with one Persona. You might have had answers in a couple of Personas—or even in all of them. That's perfectly natural. Everyone has a main, or primary, Fashion Persona. Most girls also have a secondary Persona or two. Why is that?

One reason is your schedule is packed with different activities at different times of the day or year. You feel more comfortable with different Personas at various times. For example, when getting ready for school, the Natural Persona might fit that situation better. Maybe you'd rather sleep an extra fifteen minutes than deal with makeup or any hairstyle more complicated than a pony-tail. But on weekends, when you attend religious services, go out with friends, or have other plans,

and you aren't as rushed, you might favor the Classic or Romantic looks of skirts and dresses.

A Romantic girl might have Trend Tracker influences. She loves to shop and study what music and movie celebri-ties are wearing. If she sees one of her favorites wearing a denim jacket, which usually isn't a Romantic choice, she might want to adopt that look. But she'll tone down the rug-gedness of the jacket by pairing it with a lace or velveteen skirt.

Another time Personas overlap is when new fashion trends and fads appear. It's normal to want to wear what other girls and older sisters are wearing and to feel like you're a part of the latest thing. It's okay to adopt a new trend or fad once in a while just for the fun of it.

Let's say that rhinestone flip-flops are suddenly big at your school. You usually don't wear flip-flops because the strap hurts when it rubs between your toes. You like ballet flats. But your friends buy rhinestone flip-flops, so you do too. After all, they are cute and cheap. If you really want them and have the money, go ahead. Enjoy your purchase. But know that it's only a short-term thing. Your primary Fashion Persona hasn't changed over one inexpensive pair of flip-flops. You know who you really are. Or maybe there is another kind of sandal that you like, and you can glue rhinestones onto the straps.

Another example is the motorcycle jacket, a slim-fitting, front-zip jacket with pointed collar that is extremely popular. It's a style that every Persona can wear in one form or another. Naturals wear a motorcycle jacket in denim. Classics choose solid black, navy, or tan. Romantics might wear solid white, pastel, or a printed fabric, trimmed with a small row of lace or ruffles on the collar and cuffs.

Dramatics go for solid or shiny black with hardware detailing. Trend Trackers opt for a bright jewel color, hopefully with a designer logo.

Here's how we deal with our primary and secondary personas: Both of us are mainly Classics. If we were invited to a casual home party, we might both wear fitted, neatly ironed, dark-navy jeans and black tops. The tops are where we express our very different secondary personas. Jackie leans toward the Dramatic. She will wear a sparkly black top and accessorize with a chunky silver bracelet and a large silver pendant hanging from a choker necklace. Pamela, whose secondary persona is Romantic, will wear a black lace top and several thin gold chains. Both of us might wear a pretty ballet flat or low-heeled black boot with black fishnet stockings. We make the Classic persona work for our distinct personalities.

Experiment, we say. Try on all the Personas that

appeal to you. Eventually, one will come out as the strongest. You'll know it because it's the one you fall back on most of the time. It's the one you feel most comfortable with. It's the one you wear when no one is watching. It's the one that always feels the best.

SHARE YOUR THOUGHTS

Let's help you define your secondary Fashion Persona or Personas. Think about the clothes in your wardrobe and answer the following questions in your notebook or on your computer.

What is your primary Fashion Persona?

What is/are your secondary Fashion Persona(s)?

Describe an outfit you wore that combined your primary and secondary Fashion Personas.

Most girls own at least one item that suits each Fashion Persona. Name an item each for Classic, Natural, Romantic, Dramatic, and Trend Tracker. (If you're not sure, keep reading and come back to this later.)

12

Help! I Still Can't Find My Fashion Persona!

You always had the power.

—GLINDA THE GOOD WITCH

By now, many of you readers have identified both your primary and your secondary Fashion Personas. But what if you haven't? What if you relate more or less evenly to all the Personas—or to none of them? Does that mean you don't have a Fashion Persona? Absolutely not! Everyone has Fashion Personas, even you. We promise. Just stay with us.

Right now you could be a Mood Dresser, which is a transition stage before discovering your Fashion Persona. Mood Dressers are often confused about what to wear, and they don't have a lot of confidence in their ability to choose clothing that looks good and feels good. They try a lot of different looks, but they don't have a consistent pattern. One week they wear tailored, preppy clothes—such as khaki pants, pinstriped shirts, a blazer, and loafers—and the next week, they put on ruffled skirts and sequined T-shirts, like a Romantic might. It's okay to experiment, but only if you feel secure and confident that you are wearing exactly what you want to wear. Mood Dressers generally don't feel that way.

There are several problems to being a Mood Dresser. One, it's expensive. Because Mood Dressers don't have a defined look, they buy many different pieces in hopes of finding something that is pleasing for longer than a few hours or days. When they don't, they buy even more pieces. They often choose whatever strikes their fancy without giving much thought to building a versatile, cohesive wardrobe. They have bulging closets but claim to have nothing to wear. Another problem with Mood Dressing is it takes more time to get dressed. They may look to friends for advice, or they have to find out what everyone else is wearing to an event before deciding for themselves. Sometimes getting ready is such a challenge, they put off making decisions about what to wear. As a result, they are often late, or at the last minute they have to put something on that they don't like. Then they feel even worse. It's a vicious cycle. It's no fun, either. We are firm believers that clothes should be fun.

We have good news for you: if you are a Mood Dresser, you aren't stuck forever. Deep down, you really do have a primary Fashion Persona and perhaps one or two secondary Personas. First, let's see if you could be a Mood Dresser. Are any of the following statements true for you? If so, keep reading, and we'll show you how to get out of this transition stage and on to discovering your Fashion Persona:

* You can never find anything to wear, even though your closet is full.

* You often ask friends for fashion advice.

* Sometimes you can't decide what to wear.

* You often feel you wore the "wrong" thing.

* You have no idea what your fashion style is.

* Every week or month, you have a new fashion style.

* You change clothes several times before settling on an outfit.

* Sometimes peer pressure influences your style choices.

* You change your hairstyle often.

* Sometimes your friends or family tell you what to wear, and you do.

The following story illustrates how Zara overcame her Mood Dressing tendencies.

Zara's Story
Always Late for Important Dates

. . . .

For Zara's twelfth birthday, her parents planned a family dinner at her favorite Italian restaurant. Zara was excited, but she couldn't decide what to wear. Should it be her black-and-white polka-dotted dress with patterned tights and a ruffled cardigan? Or her animal print leggings with matching scarf and a tunic-length T-shirt with a peace sign emblem? She was still standing in front of her closet when she heard Dad honking the horn. Everyone was in the car, waiting for her to show up.

Finally, she put on her navy-and-pink romper, wide brown belt, and a washed denim jacket. It took her so long to get ready that the restaurant gave away their reservation. The family had to wait a long time to get seated. It wasn't the first time Zara was late. All her friends, family, and teachers lectured her about her tardiness. Zara felt bad, but she didn't know what to do.

"My problem isn't that I don't have enough clothes," she told her mom. "I have too many clothes, and I think about them a lot."

Mom suggested a new strategy: The night before school and other events, when she had plenty of time, Zara was to pull out two complete outfits she was satisfied with. Then, when she was getting dressed, she only had to choose between two looks—not an entire closet. Zara gave it a try. Not only did her on-time record improve, but she gained more confidence in her wardrobe skills. After several tries, she realized she felt best wearing her prettiest, most girly clothes rather than the up-to-the-minute trendier ones. Having fewer choices led her to see she is a Romantic. Now when she goes shopping, she looks at those styles first.

If you believe you are a Mood Dresser, here are the steps for getting out of the transition stage and on to the real you:

1. Study. If you wanted to learn a new dance step, what would you do? You would study someone doing it. You would break down the movements while counting out the beats, over and over. Then you would try it out slowly and gradually build up speed. After enough tries, you wouldn't even have to think about the steps anymore—you would just be dancing.

   Fashion coordination works the same way. Study store windows and magazines to learn what the

103

experts have paired together. Some stores give back-to-school fashion shows, where you can see the styles that are coming up. Others present color or theme collections where every top goes with every bottom. Read a fashion magazine every month. When an outfit catches your eye, rate it with one star for Like, two stars for Really Like, and three stars for Love It. After three months, study your three-star ratings. What are the similarities? Make a poster, or vision board, of your three-star picks, and hang it on your closet door as a guide.

2. Make clothing combinations from the pieces you own. Once a week, create a few outfits for the various places you will be going. Try them on to be sure they fit well and are clean. This is your dress rehearsal.

3. Take a photograph. When you put together an outfit you really like, document it! The next time you start

to feel undecided, look through those photos with confidence that each outfit is a winning combination.

4. Ask someone whose advice you trust and who won't make fun of you. Does this print top go with these capris? Does this denim vest go with this striped shirt? Should I wear the tank over the T-shirt or under it? Is this pom-pom hair clip too much?

5. Organize. After you are sure your outfits are well composed, hang them in one area of your closet alongside the appropriate accessories.

6. Give yourself time. Don't rush yourself in the morning. Set your alarm clock fifteen minutes earlier than usual so you have enough time to get dressed and make any last-minute changes.

7. Take one last glance in the mirror and congratulate yourself on how great you look! Simply awesome.

8. Keep learning. As you narrow down the clothes you love and feel good about wearing, patterns emerge. Compare them to the Fashion Persona Quiz and descriptions of the Personas until you can make a match or two.

9. Repeat. Repeat. Repeat.

While you are working on finding your Fashion Persona, consider the following shopping and coordination tips:

* Try not to shop with friends, especially if you are easily influenced by them. Your Fashion Personas are not the same. Shop only with someone who understands your Fashion Persona.

* Always shop with a list, so you aren't tempted to pick items that won't go with anything you own. It's okay to list a couple of silly things once in a while, as long as you have the basics covered.

* Don't buy it unless you have at least three things at home that you can wear it with.

* Keep your accessories simple. Don't try too hard to mix and match unrelated items. For example, if you plan to wear your leather jewelry, just stick to that. Don't add your big plastic flower ring and rhinestone headband.

* If you ever have to choose an outfit without any time, pick something Classic. It's the Fashion Persona look that is most appropriate for every occasion. You'll never go wrong.

* Take up a hobby or activity, like sports or music or scrapbooking. Get really involved. As you get better and better at it, your confidence builds. That confidence carries over into your fashion decisions.

Classics, Trends, and Fads— What's the Difference?

Before we go any farther, you need to know the difference between *classics*, *trends*, and *fads*. These terms refer to very different fashion forms.

Classics are forever. They are in style year after year, although some of the details will change. Jeans, for example, are a classic. They have been around since Levi Strauss began manufacturing the Levi's brand in 1873. Tan trench coats, T-shirts, khaki pants, cardigan sweaters, and penny loafers are other classics.

Trends are styles that are popular for several years. Then they move into fashion history books—for a short time or forever. Bell-bottom jeans were popular in the 1960s and 1970s, were replaced by jeans with tightly rolled ankles in the 1980s, and then came back into style in the 1990s. You may see your mom wearing jackets, sweaters, and shirts with shoulder pads in many years' worth of photos, but does she wear them now?

Fad is an acronym that stands for the phrase "For a Day." Fads come and go quickly. Their lifespan could be a few weeks to a few months. Fads are usually quirky, visible, and fun. Then the novelty wears off, and people look for the next new thing. Floral-print jeans are a current fad. They are just so memorable that you don't want to wear them very often. If you happen to miss out on a fad—say, glow-in-the-dark sunglasses or teddy bear backpacks—no worries. Another one will come along very soon.

"Fashions fade. Style is eternal."
—Yves Saint Laurent

You might be interested to know that some trends and fads get started by tweens. Rainbow-colored nail polish is a big one. For decades (ask your grandmother), fashion dictated that women and girls sport a limited range of polish colors: red, pink, peach, nude, and clear. Then the blues and greens and yellows and blacks came out. The only customers to embrace them were the youngest—girls like you! They were Expressionistas. Today, women of all ages are flaunting a wide range of artwork on their fingernails.

Just think: you can be a national trendsetter!

SHARE YOUR THOUGHTS

In your notebook or on your computer, write your thoughts about classics, fads, and trends. Your answers will help you further develop your sense of style.

Do you prefer to wear classics, trends, or fads?

Why?

What fads are going on at your school right now?

Do you follow the fads?

What fad(s) have you enjoyed the most?

DRESS TO EXPRESS

It's perfectly fine to follow a fad once in a while. Just know that a fad item is a short-term purchase, so you don't want to spend a lot. Put the biggest chunk of your money into classics (for whatever Persona you are!). In the long run, classics cost the least because you wear them the most.

✺

13

Every Fashion Persona Can Wear Everything

Make it work.

—TIM GUNN

*W*e hope you're not thinking, "I'm a Natural. I can't ever wear anything sparkly or fun." Please don't. It's just not true. Every Fashion Persona can wear anything. Any style. Any trend. Any look. So, you Natural girls are not locked into a lifetime of denim and fleece. Romantics aren't stuck wearing only lace and ruffles. A Classic is free to choose a lime raincoat, and a Dramatic can wear a plain, navy T-shirt dress. It's all a matter of how you put together your look. The lime-green raincoat might be the Classic's one bold purchase for the season. The Dramatic might top the navy T-shirt dress with a bold print jacket, a yellow leather belt, and red kitten-heel

111

shoes. And we know plenty of Natural girls who keep their toenails polished for the pool and the track, but they would never paint their fingernails.

Let's use lace as an example. Every Fashion Persona can wear lace in some shape or form if she wants to, not just the Romantics. Lace comes in so many types: thin strips, wide strips, flat, ruffled, white, beige, and every color of the rainbow. It comes see-through and it comes with a lining. Lace can be a tiny accent or it can be an entire dress.

Here are some of the ways that each Fashion Persona can put some lace into her wardrobe:

Classics can wear blouses with lace collars or tie a lacy scarf around their necks. A Classic whose personality runs toward the Dramatic can wear a lace jacket in whatever color suits her.

Naturals can wear lace-edged camisoles or tank tops either alone or layered under another shirt. They can wear a denim skirt with a row of lace at the hem, and they can anchor their ponytails with lacy hairclips.

Romantics wear lots of small lace, usually as a trim, but perhaps a lace blouse or lace skirt would add some oomph.

Dramatics can wear lots of lace, big lace, and colored lace, like a ruffled lace skirt, jeans with lace appliqués, or a red lace coat.

Trend Trackers wear lace if they see it on their favorite celebrities or role models, and then find a way to put their own special spin on it. (And then they're off, on to something else.)

DO IT WITH DENIM

Isn't it fun to apply fashion trends to all the Personas? You can get really creative. Plus, it's important to learn to recognize *all* the Fashion Personas, not just yours. That's the key to understanding the girls and women in our lives and having better relationships with them. So let's do another one. How about denim? Denim is usually a Natural's favorite fabric, but every Persona can wear it. And they all do. Take a look:

CLASSICS: They love denim because it's so versatile. They can wear it in many ways: shirts, dresses, long skirts, miniskirts, jackets, cut-off shorts, and pants. What they don't do is wear their denim in a loud way. No big logos or designs, and not too tight.

Typical Look: boot-cut jeans with solid, checked, or striped shirt; a navy V-neck tennis sweater, perhaps draped across her shoulders with the arms tied together in front; leather loafers, tennis shoes, or flats; a solid leather handbag or wristlet; gold stud earrings.

NATURALS: They wear whatever easy-fitting jeans they love. Usually straight legged and sometimes made from a stretchy denim. Comfort is more important than fashion flair.

Typical Look: relaxed jeans with a zip-front sweatshirt hoodie in gray, white, or black; a solid-color T-shirt or a couple of layered tank tops; athletic-style shoes, maybe high-tops; a backpack, no purse.

ROMANTICS: They wear denim skirts, perhaps trimmed in lace or with appliqués. If they wear jeans, the rest of their outfit is soft and girly.

Typical Look: jeans or jeggings worn with a pink floral top and a white, crocheted shrug; ballerina flats and a headband with a

flower decoration; a Hello Kitty or floral-print backpack and wallet; small pearl earrings or dainty gold hoops and a locket necklace.

DRAMATICS: They wear colored denim, jeans with extreme styling like rips and leather (real or faux) trim, oversize jean jackets, or anything that gets them noticed.

Typical Look: bell-bottom jeans, perhaps ripped, studded around the pockets and down the sides; a metallic tank top and emerald-green velour baseball jacket; platform sandals or short boots; chunky plastic bracelet and necklace and big hoop earrings; a large denim shoulder bag.

TREND TRACKERS: They follow whatever and whoever is hot this season.

Typical Look: whatever the magazine covers and new music videos suggest—which her imagination then moves forward!

NOW YOU DO IT

Crochet is a regular fashion trend that we see in dresses, vests, shrugs, jewelry, and many other forms. Based on your knowledge of Fashion Personas, what are the possibilities for each Persona—Classic, Natural, Romantic, Dramatic, and Trend Tracker—to be part of this trend? Compare your ideas, which you can write in your notebook or on your computer, to ours: Classics could use a crocheted shoulder bag or clutch; Naturals, a hobo bag, a vest, or even a skirt if it looks hippie-ish; Romantics, a sweater or shrug

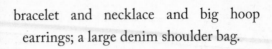

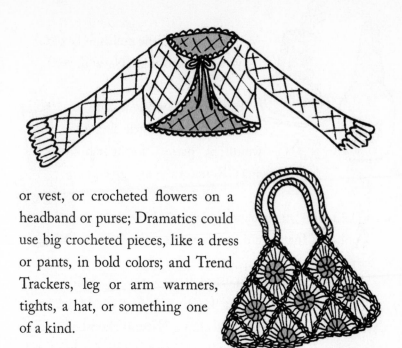

or vest, or crocheted flowers on a headband or purse; Dramatics could use big crocheted pieces, like a dress or pants, in bold colors; and Trend Trackers, leg or arm warmers, tights, a hat, or something one of a kind.

TRY IT WITH NAIL POLISH

Each Persona treats her fingernails differently. There are many possibilities: no polish, light polish, bright polish, crazy polish, and so on.

Which of the five main Fashion Personas would wear black and silver crackle polish? (Dramatic would!)

Which Persona would say, "Bright orange is so hot!" (Trend Tracker might know that orange is right on trend.)

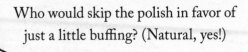

Who would skip the polish in favor of just a little buffing? (Natural, yes!)

Pale pink, with a flower painted on one little finger, would be perfect for which Persona? (Romantic—we agree.)

And who might choose clear or skin-toned polish? (That would fit Classic to a T.)

You can do this exercise with any item of clothing, cosmetic, or hairstyle. What kind of T-shirt would a Classic wear? What kind of boot would a Natural choose? For fun, go through a catalog, maybe a shoe catalog. Look at each pair of shoes and decide which Fashion Persona would wear it. Then take it a step further and say, "My mom is a Natural, so she would like these black-and-gray rubber rain boots" and "My cousin Tabitha is a Dramatic who would wear these knee-high gladiator sandals."

BE CREATIVE AND FLEXIBLE

What if you're a Romantic who doesn't like lace? Or a Natural who isn't into denim and jeans? No problem. Just skip it. No one says you *must* wear lace or jeans. Our descriptions of the Fashion Personas are guidelines and generalizations, not rigid rules. Expressionistas have many choices. Instead of jeans, Natural girls can try leggings or cargo pants or kha-kis or cozy yoga pants. The big idea is to know what you feel good wearing and find all the ways you can to express who you are, not what somebody else is or what you think you should be. So don't stress if you don't fit perfectly into a certain Persona. Almost no one does. The important thing to remember is: Every Fashion Persona can wear anything she wants. She'll just do it in her own special way. The Expressionista way.

Tips

Fashion Personas for
Every Body Shape and Image

Expressionistas come in a wide range of shapes and sizes. Some are tall and thin. Some are tall and muscular. Some of them are petite. That's so okay. Young bodies go through many physical and emotional changes. All of the changes are normal and natural, including the confusing and embarrassing ones. Stay true to your Fashion Persona, and you will know you look great, even when you don't feel so wonderful on the inside.

"There are actresses who build themselves, and then there are actresses who are built by others. I want to build myself."

—JENNIFER LAWRENCE

No matter what your size and Fashion Persona, you can wear all the latest styles you want. Today, every fashion design and trend is made for all body types. Jeans are designed for skinny legs and wide legs, high waists and low waists, and in comfortable stretch fabrics. Swimwear styles include itsy-bitsy bikinis, but swim dresses and board shorts not only cover more skin, but are much more in style these days. As for tunics and other tops, pretty draping, ruching, and ruffles flatter well-endowed chests as well as smaller ones.

Once you know your Fashion Persona, don't let anyone influence you away from it, certainly not celebrity magazines and high-fashion glamour photography. The faces and bodies you see have been styled and airbrushed to create fantasy, not reality. And Barbie? If she were a real woman, she would be seven feet tall, weigh a hundred pounds, and have a nineteen-inch waist! In other words, she wouldn't be alive, let alone be able to stand!

EXPRESSIONISTA QUOTE:

"Don't get paranoid about your size."

The reality is that many modern-day female role models—Jennifer Hudson and Kate Upton, to name a couple—have realistic shapes. The ultrafamous Kardashian sisters are ultracurvy—and proud of it. In the modeling world, there are bans on very young models and very thin models.

Perhaps you have stood in front of a mirror at home or in a store and wished that you could be taller, slimmer, curvier, or even someone else. We hope you don't. Expressionistas know there is no such thing as a bad body. It's just that the clothes you may be picking out are totally wrong for the shape of your body. We give a letter designation to the most common shapes: Y, i, I, A, and X. Just like Fashion Personas, every letter or body shape can wear every style. But certain details and silhouettes are more flattering to certain body shapes. Here we describe the various letter designations and provide style tips for them. Remember, just like Fashion Personas, all body shapes are perfect.

Y: The Y shape is fuller on the top than on the bottom. Sometimes Ys feel self-conscious about their maturing shapes. It's not necessary to feel that way when they know how to flatter.

* Don't over cover. Too much fabric on top makes you look larger.

* Choose tops with scoop necks or small V-necks to bring attention to your face rather than your chest. Wear structured rather than clingy fabrics.

* Bell-bottom and wide-legged pants help balance the spaces above and below your waist.

* Knee-length or below-the-knee skirts add bottom weight. If you love short skirts, choose patterns, prints, and tiers.

i: The lower-case i is the petite figure. She may wish for the stature of supermodels, but she can wear anything they wear as long as the pieces are proportioned to her smaller frame.

* Avoid cuffs on your pants or shorts because they make you appear shorter.

* Pair your pants and jeans with the same color socks and shoes to elongate your legs.

* Tops should come to your waist. Longer lengths visually shorten your legs.

* Keep skirt lengths just below the knee and shorter. Midcalf skirts make you seem smaller.

I: The capital I shape is tall and of any width. The I shape may be self-conscious if she towers over everyone at a young age, but she eventually learns to love those inches!

* Look for pants and jeans that are available in long lengths. Ankle-length pants are popular if they were designed that way, but generally you want your pant hems to hug your shoes.

* Cut your height by wearing different colors on top and bottom. Belts have the same effect.

* Tuck in your shirts and T-shirts to define your waist.

* Full skirts and flared pants add visual weight to your bottom half.

A: The A shape is fuller below the waist than above it. She often worries about her hips appearing large. This is not the case when she knows how to balance her clothing pieces.

* Select flat-front or slim-legged pants in longer lengths. Avoid side pockets, which have a widening effect.

* Choose hip-length tops and jackets to elongate your upper body. Scarves add visual weight on top.

* Keep your tops and bottoms in the same color family for a leaner look. Wear the brightest colors and prints on top.

* Flared skirts cover. Wear oversize tops with slim skirts.

X: The X shape is curvy, with a small waist and a larger top and bottom. She can show off her waistline, but too much cinching may exaggerate the other parts.

* Buy jeans with a hint of spandex for comfort and flattery.

* Wear straight-legged pants in dark colors for a streamlined effect.

* Keep belts in the same color as the rest of your outfit.

* Patterned or decorated tops ending at the waist or slightly below take the focus off your bottom.

As you grow up, your body continually changes its shape. You might grow taller or not. You might grow rounder or thinner. Your Fashion Persona stays the same (although your primary and secondary Personas may shift). Read how Tara dealt with her love of fashion while going through a dramatic change of her body shape:

Tara's Story
Focus on Accessories

* *

Tara is a third-grade schoolteacher now, but she was an overweight child and teen. She always planned to lose weight, and eventually she did. She lost eighty pounds while she was in college by following the Weight Watchers program, and she has kept the weight off. While Tara was heavy, she did not buy many clothes, especially not costly designer pieces. Mostly she wore inexpensive jeans and T-shirts. Instead, she invested in good accessories and asked that family members do the same when buying her gifts. She always carried leather purses, and she wore a small diamond pendant and 14-karat gold earrings with garnets (her birthstone). She also became a wizard at knotting and tying gorgeous scarves. No matter what her weight, these pieces always fit. They helped her portray an image of class, and they last a lifetime.

Expressionistas love ourselves just the way we are. We are so busy living our lives that we don't fall for peer criticism or media hype. Outsiders can't destroy the confidence we have in ourselves. Here's what we know:

* Fashion Persona is more significant than body shape or size.

* Healthy is more important than thin.

* Only your doctor can determine if you need to lose weight.

* Eating healthy foods and being physically active is important.

* Everyone should avoid extremes—meaning no fad diets and no crazy exercise routines.

> **INSIDER TIP:**
>
> Jeans can be especially hard to fit because you're still growing. Try all the departments (girls, juniors, misses, and even boys) and all the different cuts (boot cut, flare, high waisted, boyfriend, and so on).

* If you don't love your body right now, you can start by loving what your body can do. Can you ride a skateboard, play the violin, kick a soccer ball, style your hair, play computer games, or hold your baby sister's hand?

* You should embrace your Fashion Persona and love her.

Test Your Knowledge of Fashion Personas

Let's see how much you have learned about the different Fashion Personas. Remember that you want to know all the Personas, so you can relate to them in a more meaningful way. In this quiz, we tell you how six young girls dressed for an event. Your assignment is to figure out the Persona of each one. Write your answers in your notebook or on your computer. If you need help, we have provided answers at the end.

Lila is going to her favorite cousin's twelfth birthday party at a Chinese restaurant. It's a girls-only gathering that includes several classmates and two more cousins. Lila loves sweet-and-sour shrimp and fried rice. She's decided to wear a short, ruffled denim skirt with navy-blue lace tights, a white shirt with little pearl buttons and a lace collar, and a pink shrug. She chooses pearl stud earrings and a pearl bracelet to match her shirt, and her black suede boots. For her hair, she clips back the sides and top with a barrette with long ribbons.

What is Lila's Fashion Persona?

Madison is going to the movies on a Saturday afternoon with her two best friends. They can walk to the theater, which is only a few blocks from their neighborhood. Madison wears her new black jeggings, layered tank tops in red and white, and a gray hoodie imprinted with her school's name. Her shoes are black, low-rise basketball shoes. For jewelry, she chooses tiny silver hoop earrings and a thin silver bracelet, and she slips her money into a small wristlet bag.

What is Madison's Fashion Persona?

Cassie will be attending her school's year-end dance. It's a huge event because she'll be a freshman next year. Some, but not all, of her friends are going to the same high school. The dance is one of the last times they will all be together. Cassie wants to make sure everyone remembers her. Here's what she decides to wear: a white taffeta dress with a row of silvery ribbon at the neck, waist, and hem; silver shoes with kitten heels; a ruffled gold hair ornament to tie her hair into a side ponytail; her mom's crystal bead necklace; and her beloved Hello Kitty sequined purse.

What is Cassie's Fashion Persona?

Jadie is going to the same school dance as Cassie, but she isn't sure what she will wear. She waits until the day of the dance and then changes her clothes several times. She settles on her best dress: black velvet and long sleeves, even though it's hot outside. She borrows a pair of white lace tights from her older sister. The tights are a little big, but they will have to do. She'll run to the bathroom to pull them up all night. Fortunately, the accessorizing goes easily: black flats, a gold locket necklace, small dangly earrings, and a black leather minibag. Now she has to hurry—her stepdad is already in the car, honking the horn. It's time to go!

What is Jadie's Fashion Persona?

Macy and her parents spend the weekend at her brother's college. She is very excited to be attending her first college football game. The weather is cold, but she's ready. She wears straight-legged jeans with a navy-and-white striped sweater. She tops that with a green puffer vest and a long knit scarf and navy mittens. She adds her tan, fleece-lined low boots.

What is Macy's Fashion Persona?

Grace attends a school that requires students to wear uniforms, but the girls find ways to show their individuality. The uniform is a white blouse and a navy-and-forest plaid jumper. A navy cardigan can be added for cooler weather. One day, Grace puts a hot-pink ruffled tank under her white blouse and unbuttons the top button, so the tank peeks through. Her school doesn't allow any logos or brand names, so Grace makes sure to hide the logo on her tank. Then she adds a hot-pink ruffled bow to her ponytail. She also wears pink socks with her black Mary Jane shoes. Her backpack is a deep orange hue—that's Grace's favorite new color of the season. She also wears a small silver locket from a fancy jewelry store that her parents gave her for her last birthday.

What is Grace's Fashion Persona?

Answers: Lila is a Romantic; Madison is a Classic; Cassie is a Dramatic; Jadie is a Mood Dresser; Macy is a Natural; Grace is a Trend Tracker.

14

Closetology 101

The mirror can lie.
It doesn't show you
what's inside.

—DEMI LOVATO

Closetology is the science of choosing the clothing
pieces and accessories that make you feel good on
the inside and give you the confidence on the outside to live
your life.

Your closet is not just space that holds clothes. It is a place
you visit every time you need to choose something to wear for
every activity of every day and every week. Visiting it should
be a peaceful activity, not a scavenger hunt. Your closet (and
dresser drawers and other storage compartments) should be
organized in ways that make clothing selection easy and

stress free. That's the key to knowing if you have the pieces you need and to locating them when you do.

Our goal in this chapter is to help you excel in your personal Closetology. The first step is to get your closet working for you. Then we can identify what you have and what you might need.

Start by answering yes or no to the following questions in your notebook or on your computer:

Do you feel good about your closet?

Are you embarrassed for someone else to see your closet?

Do you wear more than 50 percent of the pieces hanging there?

Can you easily see everything in your closet?

Have any clothes fallen off the hangers and onto the floor?

Are your winter clothes separate from your summer clothes?

Does every piece of clothing in your closet fit you?

Do you like every piece of clothing you own?

Do you know what is at the back of your closet?

Is your closet packed so tightly that things fall out when you open the door?

EXPRESSIONISTA
QUOTE:

"Don't be afraid to try new things."

If you don't like your answer to any of the above questions, read on for suggestions and ideas to improve your Closetology. Even if your closet, and your attitude about it, seems to be in pretty good shape, you are sure to pick up many great pointers from our eight-step action plan.

Step 1: Twice a year, at the beginning of spring and fall, make a date with yourself to visit your closet with a critical eye.

Step 2: Do you live in an area that has warm and cold seasons? If so, in the spring, put all your cold-weather clothing at the back of your closet. The idea is to get those items out of the way, so you can work on your warm-weather pieces. (Repeat this step in the fall with your warm-weather clothes.)

Step 3: Arrange your clothing into classifications: Hang pants with pants, skirts with skirts, tops with tops, and jackets with jackets. Remember to hang only one garment per hanger, so you don't hide or lose any pieces. Then, gather up all your shoes and place them side by side. Check out your socks too, to make sure they have mates.

> DRESS TO EXPRESS
> FOR CLOSETOLOGY
>
> *After your clothes are grouped by type, arrange each classification by color, from light to dark.*

Step 4: Go through each grouping and look at each piece. Try it on in front of your mirror. Ask these questions:

* Do I still like this piece?

* Do I absolutely love it, or do I hate it?

134

* Do I wear it a lot?

* Does it fit me?

* Does it need to be laundered?

* Does it need repair?

* Have I worn it in the last year?

Step 5: Now go through all of your accessories and ask the same questions.

Step 6: Make three piles on the floor: One pile is for items that need to be cleaned. One is for items that need repair. One is for items you don't wear for whatever reason.

Step 7: Clean the pieces that need cleaning and fix the pieces that need fixing. Return them to your closet.

As for the ones you don't wear, ask yourself why for each piece. Think about your answer and don't say you don't know. Is it too tight? Too short? Too scratchy? Did someone make a nasty remark about it? Does it work with your Fashion Persona? Can you make it work?

> INSIDER TIP:
>
> *Dress for action when you know you will be trying on clothes. Wear things that are easy to take off and on—slip-on shoes and no layers, so you don't spend a lot of time fussing.*

If something is truly hopeless, you have choices: Donate it to a charity. Hand it down to a sister or cousin. Sell it at a tween resale shop. (You'll earn more money there than if you try to sell it at a garage sale.) Or have a swap party with friends. The pale-green denim jacket you aren't wearing may be a piece a friend would love to have. From time to time, you will come across a piece of clothing that no longer fits but is too

special to get rid of, and you don't have room in your closet to keep things you can't or don't wear. Put them in a pretty box or storage bag and tuck that under your bed. (Pamela still has a skirt she embroidered when she was in third grade—it's in a box on the top shelf of the guest-room closet.)

Step 8: Congratulate yourself on a job well done. Your clothes are now in tip-top shape, and you know which ones you love and which ones you don't. But we're not done yet. The next chapter helps you fine tune your closet and dresser so you can always find what you want.

15

Avoid Closet Chaos: Tips and Tricks for Setting Up Your Closet

If you believe in yourself,
you can be anything.

—KATY PERRY

Where's my pink hoodie?"

"Those are my jeans, not yours. Take them off right now or I'm telling Mom."

"The cat slept on my cheerleading shirt and got hair all over it."

"I can't find my other running shoe!"

"I don't have anything to wear."

"What did you do with my strawberry lip gloss?"

"My ski jacket was on the blue chair in the den when I saw it last."

Do any of these sound familiar? If they do, you have Closet Chaos. No wonder getting dressed is a chore. Your clothes, accessories, and makeup are spread all over the house. You're running around, looking for your stuff. Next thing you know, you're late for your ride. You settle for something you don't want to wear, or you don't have time for breakfast. It's not a good way to start off the day.

Expressionistas keep our wardrobes organized, even if we don't own a lot of clothes. Organization is the key to our creativity. When everything is arranged neatly, an Expressionista knows exactly where to find her butterfly T-shirt, black jeggings, and crocheted vest. And she has more time to experiment with more combos.

Let's see if you have Closet Chaos.

. . . .

QUIZ

Do You Have Closet Chaos?

. . . .

* Do you have trouble finding things you want in your closet?

* Do you hang more than one item on a hanger?

* Are your pants, tops, and dresses all mixed together in your closet?

* Do your clothes ever look wrinkled when you put them on?

* Are your shoes located in several different places around the house?

* Is any of your jewelry tangled or knotted up?

* If you had a sleepover tonight, would you know where your favorite pj's are?

* Do you ever lose pieces of clothing?

* Is your soccer uniform or choir robe ready for the next game or performance?

* Are there clothes under your bed? (We're not talking about out-of-season pieces that are stored neatly.)

INSIDER TIP:

Try on everything before you buy. Sizes vary from store to store and from brand to brand.

If you answered yes to any of these questions, you are headed for serious Closet Chaos!

Dress to Express for Closets

The following tips and tricks will put your closet in tip-top shape. When it is, getting dressed will be so much easier.

* Buy matching hangers for a neater appearance.

* Turn hangers so they face the same direction.

* Place only one item per hanger.

* Hang similar items together: dresses, skirts, pants, jeans, blouses, and tops. Then arrange each category by color, from light to dark.

* T-shirts, sweaters, and sweatshirts can be hung on hangers or folded in your dresser, wherever you have more space.

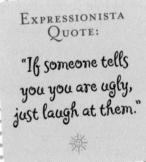

EXPRESSIONISTA QUOTE:

"If someone tells you you are ugly, just laugh at them."

* Fold and stack your sweaters by type: long sleeved, short sleeved, cardigan, summer weight, winter weight.

* If your closet is really small, store out-of-season pieces under the bed neatly in bags or boxes.

* If you share a closet with a sibling, keep your clothes on one side and hers on the other to keep them separate. Draw or tape a dividing line. You could even paint each side a different color if your parents approve.

* Separate white socks and colored socks.

* Arrange your shoes in pairs and stand them side by side. No tossing them in a heap at the bottom of your closet!

EXPRESSIONISTA
QUOTE:

"I like all my clothes because I bought them."

* Buy or make some decorative boxes: use one for hair accessories, one for jewelry, and another for sunglasses.

* Make a gorgeous wall display of your hats!

* Use milk crates and wall pegs for extra storage space.

* Separate items you don't wear often, like Halloween costumes or your band uniform. If you don't have another closet to use, hang them in the back. Don't mix them with your daily clothes—you'll start to lose things.

* Make repairs as soon as you notice them. It's easy to forget, and if you do, the next time you want to wear that piece of clothing, you won't have time to stitch a tear or replace a button. You'll feel stressed, and that's not a good way to start your day.

* Before you leave the house, check yourself in a full-length mirror.

Expressionista Assignment: In your notebook or on your computer, list three steps you need to take to organize your clothes. Now name the date you will finish the three steps you listed above.

16

Expressionista Fashion Math: The Secret Formula

This is the body you've been given—love what you've got.

—OPRAH WINFREY

Would you like to own way more clothes than you do now? Wouldn't that solve the annoying problem of never having anything to wear? That's the way many girls (and women) think. Well, it's just not true. First of all, if you had all the clothes and shoes and purses and scarves you ever wanted, where would you put them? You would have them all over your bedroom and your house and probably some in the basement and in the attic, and then it would be hard to find your lime-green ballet flats with the black sequined flower on the toes when you want them. You'd spend so much time hunting down those shoes that

the party would be over before you were even dressed!

There's a much better way to have lots and lots of outfits. It's called Expressionista Fashion Math. Normally, two plus two makes four, and eleven plus eleven makes twenty-two. But using the secret formula of Expressionista Fashion Math, eight pieces of clothing can be mixed and matched to create twenty-two outfits. That means you could wear something different every single day for three weeks and have an outfit left over. Pretty amazing.

How the formula works: Choose four colors you want to build your wardrobe around. At least two of

the colors should be neutrals, such as navy, black, tan, brown, gray, beige, or white. The other two can be anything you like.

As an example, you might select blue denim, white, red, and navy blue.

Here are the eight pieces you'll need. We call this your Core Wardrobe. Each

INSIDER TIP:

Stick with two or three basic colors and a couple of accent colors so that more things go together. For example, you might choose navy and black as your basics, and purple and lime green to accessorize.

piece should be one of your four colors, but it doesn't matter which one:

1 jacket

1 pair of pants or jeans

1 additional pair of pants or a skirt

5 assorted tops (T-shirts, polos, blouses, camisoles, and so on)

Now, start making combinations:

Option One: Team the jacket with the first pants. Wear the jacket buttoned up, like a shirt.

147

Options Two through Six: Team the pants with each of the tops. Layer the unbuttoned jacket over the tops.

Options Seven through Eleven: Remove the jacket. Accessorize the tops with scarves, shrugs, shawls, or jewelry, however you wish.

Are you keeping track? You now have eleven different looks using the first seven pieces. Repeat the above options using the second pair of pants or the skirt. That's eleven more outfits.

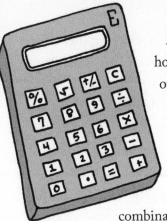

And that, dear Expressionista, is how eight pieces add up to twenty-two outfits!

You can add another core piece, perhaps a sweater twinset or a denim skirt, and watch your options grow.

Use this formula with your own wardrobe to see how many combinations you can come up with. You'll find that you have many more clothing options than you knew!

Here's some more Expressionista Fashion Math: It isn't how much you pay for a piece of clothing that makes it a value. It's how many times you wear it that counts. A $100 dress marked down to $30 might seem like a bargain, but if you wear it only once, it costs $30 per wearing. A $50 dress marked down to $40 doesn't appear to be as big a deal. But if you wear the dress once a week for three months, it costs less than $4 each time.

Expressionista Assignment: List a clothing item you recently bought or received as a gift. Then list three items from your existing wardrobe that go with each one. What two new items would help you create additional outfits? How many new outfits can you come up with?

Expressionista Assignment: Pull out three of your most beloved clothing pieces. One at a time, hold them up to everything else in your closet. Try to find two new combinations for each one. Take photos, so you don't forget about them the next time you're debating what to wear.

Expressionista Assignment: Take photographs of all your favorite outfits. Use them to create a mini-magazine with you on the cover! You're an Expressionista cover girl!

DRESS TO EXPRESS

You don't need more clothes. You need more combinations. Always buy pieces that go with things you already own.

Tips

How to Be Perfectly Mismatched

It's great fun to mix patterns, prints, and plaids for creative effect, but it takes a little effort to be good at it. Believe it or not, there are rules for looking as though you are not following any rules. First, you can't just put anything together. Only an expert stylist can assemble tiger-print pants, a camouflage T-shirt, a sequined vest, a tutu, and a turban in one outfit and make it look good.

Here are some tips for perfect mismatching:

* If you mix two floral patterns, one print should be big and one should be small.

* Use small prints that almost look like solids from far away. They mix fine with stripes and plaids.

* Add a solid jacket, vest, or wide belt to break up two prints.

* Experiment with different textures, like velvet and denim or metallic and fleece.

* Jewel tones mismatch better than pastels, which all together make you look like rainbow sherbet. Pair pale yellow with cobalt blue or soft pink with shocking orange.

EXPRESSIONISTA QUOTE:

"Sometimes my mom buys me something, and I don't like it, but a couple of days later I do."

Mismatched socks are cute but not one white athletic sock and one red-and-navy knee sock. To make a successful mismatch, the socks need a common element like length, yarn, or color. You can wear one red-and-blue knee sock with one green-and-yellow knee sock if they are the same length and yarn, or one red athletic sock and one green athletic sock.

QUIZ

What Kind of Shopper Are You?

For most young girls, shopping is great sport. For some, it is a bothersome chore. Everyone has a shopping style, just like everyone has a Fashion Persona. What kind of shopper are you? Learn more by taking this quiz. Choose the answers that fit you the best. Scoring is at the end.

1. When you visit the mall you:
   A. Go to my favorite stores and usually find what I am looking for
   B. Head for the accessories first. Headbands and hair ornaments are my signature look.
   C. Don't shop very much
   D. Go into every store and every department, looking for new things
   E. Wander the mall not knowing what to buy
   F. Take pictures from fashion magazines to guide me

2. Who do you prefer to shop with and why?
   A. My mother. We usually like the same things.
   B. My best friend. We trade clothes a lot, so we like to go together.
   C. Myself. I like the sports clothing stores best.
   D. My three best friends. I show them the newest things to buy.
   E. My cousin. We go to the mall often. She buys a lot, and I get one or two things.
   F. Myself. I like to surprise my friends with my purchases when I wear them.

3. Do you shop with a list?
   A. Sometimes—I have a pretty good idea of what I need at any time.
   B. I try to match what I have in my closet and buy one pretty new item.

C. I stick to my list.

D. I never have a list. I look for something to excite me.

E. I sometimes start out with a list, but I always return things.

F. I look for what's new. Sometimes I buy what is displayed on the mannequins.

4. Do you stick to your budget?

A. My mom gives me an idea of what I can spend.

B. I go first to look and then go back with my mom to show her what I found.

C. I don't spend much money on clothes.

D. I try to buy on sale because I want everything I see.

E. Sometimes I spend a lot, and sometimes I don't buy anything.

F. My mom says I spend too much, but I want new styles before they go on sale.

5. When you get home with your purchases you:

A. Cut off the tags and hang them up right away

B. Model them for my mom and dad so they can see how cute I look

C. Leave them in the car and run to my soccer practice

D. Experiment with different accessories I already have

E. Leave them in the bags for a few days

F. Can't wait to wear them and show off to my friends

Scoring: Add up the number of As, Bs, Cs, Ds, Es, and Fs, and write your totals down.

If you have mostly As: You are a classical shopper. You enjoy shopping, but you know your sense of style and you stick to it. You rarely regret your purchases.

If you have mostly Bs: Shopping is so much fun, especially with your best friend. You love dreaming about the clothes you hope to own someday. And you're always checking out the accessories.

If you have mostly Cs: Clearly, shopping is not your thing. You are more interested in what you are doing than what you are wearing. If you have to shop, you get it done quickly.

If you have mostly Ds: With your dramatic flair, shopping is a mission. You're always on the hunt for unique ideas and combos that will get you the most attention.

If you have mostly Es: Shopping mostly confuses you. There are so many choices, and you have to be in the right mood to find anything you like. Either that, or you like everything.

If you have mostly Fs: Shopping is your favorite pastime. You know how to take a new look and make it your own. You might have a career in the fashion industry!

17
Let's Go Shopping

I think that every teenager has a point
in their life when they go into their own
world and shut out everybody's opinion.
That's what I'm doing.

—RIHANNA

In this chapter, you will make a Master Shopping List that will be your guide for all future shopping trips. A list will make your shopping more productive, and you will be less likely to make mistakes.

Step 1: In your notebook or on your computer, make a list of all the activities and events you have coming up in the next three to six months. Here are some prompts to get you started:

157

Fall/Winter Seasons: Will you be involved in sports or musical groups that require practice or performance apparel? Will you attend any parties or sleepovers? What after-school activities or clubs do you participate in? Do you wear a uniform to school?

Spring/Summer Seasons: Will you be attending any end-of-school-year dances or graduation events? Do you and your family have vacation plans? Will you be taking any summer lessons? Will you be attending any weddings? Will you be in any weddings? Will you participate in any outdoor or recreational activities? Are you going to camp?

EXPRESSIONISTA
QUOTE:

"Don't let your friends influence you."

Step 2: Make a list of the kinds of clothing you will wear for each activity. For example:

Grandma's Birthday Party—a pretty dress with tights and ballet flats

Music Day Camp—shorts and T-shirts; khakis for last-day concert

It's okay if you don't have the exact answers for either your upcoming activities or what you will wear. Plans often change, and new plans happen at the spur of the moment. We just want you to get in the habit of thinking ahead, so you can create a flexible wardrobe with lots of possibilities. If you plan ahead, when life surprises you, you'll already have ideas of appropriate outfits.

Step 3: Now visit your closet to see how many of these items you already own and what you will need to buy.

INSIDER TIP:

When you find something that's out of your price range, ask a sales associate when it will go on sale.

Step 4: Turn to a new page and make three columns. Label the first column Basic Needs. Label the second column Wish List. Label the third column Big Dreams. Basic Needs are the must-haves of every wardrobe: athletic socks, underwear, shorts for camp, a navy T-shirt for jazz band concerts, and so on. Your Wish List is for items you see in magazines or catalogs or on someone else, and you think you might like to buy them for yourself. The Big Dreams column is for long-term purchases, maybe a designer handbag or a prom dress.

Start filling in the columns. Some Expressionistas keep their Master Shopping List in a pocket folder, so they can include pictures of clothes and accessories they want to buy or outfits they want to copy.

Step 5: Take your list with you when you shop. If you're at the mall with twenty dollars burning a hole in your pocket, and you just have to buy something, check your list. You'll satisfy the urge, but you'll also go home with something you want and can use. Cross off items as you buy them, and add more as you are inspired. The more you use your list, the fewer shopping mistakes you make. The fewer shopping mistakes you make, the more you will love your wardrobe!

Tips

Dress to Express for Shopping

* Always, always try clothes on before you buy. If you shop on the internet, make sure returns are easy.

* Buy on sale, but not *just* because something is on sale. It's no bargain if you (1) don't love it and (2) can't use it.

* Don't buy anything that doesn't go with at least three things you already own.

* Don't buy something smaller than your current size because you think it will motivate you to lose weight.

* Don't buy something because somebody else does.

* Buy what you love, not what your friends say you should buy.

* Don't wear something to impress somebody or to get them to like you.

* Don't buy anything that is hard to keep clean, like a white backpack.

* Shop with coupons—sign up on your favorite stores' websites.

* Buy what makes sense for your lifestyle and activities.

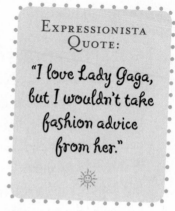

EXPRESSIONISTA QUOTE:

"I love Lady Gaga, but I wouldn't take fashion advice from her."

* Buy pieces that suit your Fashion Persona.

* If you make a shopping mistake and can't return it, pass the item along to a friend who can wear it. She'll remember you the next time she makes a mistake—and we all do from time to time!

Five Cool Places to Find New Clothes

CRAFT AND HOBBY STORES
You Can Find: T-shirts, tanks, and sweatshirts; flip-flops; feather boas; hats and caps; beads, pearls, stones, charms, jewels, appliqués, studs, sparklies, and hardware for making your own jewelry or decorating clothes and shoes.

COLLEGE BOOKSTORES
You Can Find: lots of cute sportswear and athletic wear in current colors and shapes (the goods have to be in style, or the college girls won't buy them), all decked out with the school's logo; oversize and fitted T-shirts; sweatshirts; sweatpants and shorts; jackets; headbands; caps; ear warmers, arm warmers, and leg warmers; gloves; mittens; tote bags and backpacks.

FABRIC STORES
You Can Find: T-shirts, tank tops, tote bags, headbands, hats, and flip-flops; jewelry-making kits; purse-making supplies; fabric paint in colors, metallics, and glossies; buttons, laces, ribbons, and trims; tie-dye kits; easy-to-make costumes. (Expressionistas don't need to know how to sew to create truly individual looks for themselves, but fabric stores often give lessons for beginners.)

RESALE AND CONSIGNMENT SHOPS

You Can Find: gently used clothing and accessories of all styles and sizes. Some stores are picky about the goods they carry. They might sell only newer items (no more than three years old) that are in the best condition. Their prices will be higher but still lower than stores selling brand-new merchandise. Other resale shops are like department stores: they sell everything, even kitchen sinks, and because their inventory is so huge, these shops are great for shoppers of vintage items.

GARAGE SALES

You Can Find: any kind of clothing, but especially jeans, jackets, tops, purses, and shoes; costume jewelry; items you can wear as they are, or pieces you want to take apart and make into something new.

18
Putting It All Together

Reach for the stars.

—Julianne Hough

So far, this book has been entirely about you and discovering your Fashion Persona. As you have seen, this knowledge has led to greater self-confidence and less indecision about your clothing choices. It is a tool that will guide you for all your life. But you're not done yet. It's not enough to know your own Persona. Fashion Personas are meant to be shared. As a true Expressionista, you need to know and understand *all* the Fashion Personas.

It's great fun to get together with friends and take the Fashion Persona Quiz. Discover Your Fashion Persona makes an exciting theme for a sleepover or birthday party or scout meeting. You can talk about your answers to see how you and your friends are alike and how you are different. You also can discuss how to become an Expressionista and cheer each other along the path to being one.

Knowing all the Personas also helps to improve your relationships at home and at school and at play. You'll have better understanding of why some of the people around you act the way they do. You will be able to relate to them on their levels and cut through the drama. The following stories show how different fashion personas in the same family can cause conflict or create understanding.

Emma and Ava's Story
Sisters Divided

Getting ready for school in the morning was a snap for sixth grader Emma. Every day she wore pretty much the same thing: jeans; a graphic or logo T-shirt (untucked, of course); and athletic shoes. Sometimes she wore a cap if she didn't feel like doing anything with her hair. It was more important to her that clothes were comfortable than new. In fact, she slept in one of her dad's T-shirts from high school.

Emma's older sister, Ava, was just the opposite. She loved clothes and spent hours going through magazines and websites to look for the clothes she'd like to own someday. Ava, a Trend Tracker, was always trying to show Emma new makeup tricks or inviting her to go to the mall. But Emma didn't care. She was a Natural who would rather practice her free throws with the boys on the block or help her dad in the garden. Besides, she looked just fine the way she was, Emma said as she ran out the door. Ava felt rejected by her little sister. If Ava kept on feeling rejected, permanent damage to the relationship could result.

But if Emma and Ava took the Fashion Persona Quiz together and dis- cussed their answers, they would real- ize they have very different style per- sonalities. Then they could find another com- mon ground, something they enjoy doing together, and keep the sisterly bond intact. They could enter a walkathon for a charity or volunteer at a day- care center or start

a girls' band. Emma was up for most anything, as long as it wasn't about girly clothes, and Ava would have the sisterly companionship she craved.

Ava needed to learn it was not personal—it was Fashion Personas.

Daniella's Story
Different Fashion Personas
Learn to Shop Together

• •

Fortunately, Daniella and her mother and sister were able to move past their rocky relationship that stemmed from having different Fashion Personas and interests. Thirteen-year-old Daniella was envious of the time her mother and older sister spent together. They were Romantics and loved antiques. At night, the two watched every episode of *Antiques Roadshow* and on weekends they went to flea markets and antique stores together. Daniella's mom shopped for vintage pottery, and her sister hunted for delicate jewelry. Daniella was a Dramatic who hated all that "old junk." She could hardly wait until the day she could buy her own condo and decorate it totally modern. One day Daniella's aunt gave her a beautiful gift: a glass paperweight. Daniella was fascinated by the black and gray and white and yellow swirls of color captured inside the clear orb. She decided she wanted to collect paperweights.

"I know where you might find more paperweights," her mother said.

"Where?" asked Daniella.

"At the flea market this weekend. Would you like to go with us?"

Daniella started to say no thanks, but changed her mind. She would go just once.

Sure enough, she found a paperweight—this one seemed to have a sunburst inside. It was marked ten dollars, but Daniella's mother showed her how to bargain with the dealer. She got it for seven dollars. Daniella was thrilled with her purchase. She hardly noticed when Mom said she wanted to stop at a store that carried clothing Daniella called boring. She followed her mom and sister inside, still admiring her new paperweight.

"If you see anything you like, let me know," her mom said.

Fat chance, Daniella thought. Then she spotted a black velour hoodie. It was just what she needed to go with her red skinny jeans. Her mom agreed the hoodie was cute and pulled out her credit card. Her sister got a soft, baby-blue cardigan and matching shell.

When they got home, as usual, Daniella went straight to her bedroom to be alone and listen to her beloved heavy metal music. But first she said, "If you ever see paperweights on *Antiques Roadshow*, let me know." That day was the first of many shopping trips—for antiques and for clothes—that the three enjoyed together. Their differences weren't personal; they were about Fashion Personas.

Your Expressionista and Fashion Persona skills can be applied to many situations: The new girl at your school isn't weird; she's a Trend Tracker. Your mother isn't out to ruin your life by not letting you wear crop tops and short shorts; she's a Classic who values quality, traditional clothing styles. Your cousin isn't planning a stupid camping wedding; she's a Natural who loves the outdoors and wants to be married surrounded by wildflowers on a riverbank. And she wants you to be a part of it. It's not personal; it's Fashion Personas.

Remember the second Expressionista rule of Fashion Personas: respect the Fashion Personas of others.

"I want people to see the real me."

—Miranda Cosgrove

And when anyone puts you down in some way, you know in your heart that you are an Expressionista. Hold your shoulders back and be proud of yourself. All of your life you will be criticized for one thing or another. The most beautiful, talented people in the world face huge amounts of criticism. You can't stop the haters, but you don't have to believe them. Expressionistas know who they are, and no one can take that away.

And now for your final Expressionista Assignment: Share the Fashion Persona Quiz with everyone you know and meet. Start by asking, "Do you know your Fashion Persona?" (Of course, many won't, but you've captured their interest.) Then give them the quiz. Tell them how to become an Expressionista.

Do this over and over, and your friends will do it, and their friends will do it. And then we will have entire communities of Expressionistas. Won't that be grand?

Write a big YES in your notebook or on your computer.

SHARE YOUR THOUGHTS

Tell us your Expressionista advice.

Epilogue

IN THE MIRROR AGAIN: TAKE THE EXPRESSIONISTA PLEDGE

We envision a world where every girl
knows and activates her limitless potential
and is free to boldly pursue her dreams.

—Girls on the Run International

From the beginning of this book until now, you have
been on a journey of self-discovery. You have taken
quizzes, written your innermost thoughts, and completed the
assignments. You have found your Fashion Persona, or you
are working on it. You know how to use it to love yourself
more and to relate to other people better. You have organized
your closet and have begun your Master Shopping List.

Are you an Expressionista yet? Almost. There are two parts to becoming an Expressionista: looking good on the outside and feeling good on the inside. They are related. You can wear the most amazing outfits on all the runways, but if it doesn't make you feel good on the inside, you will not be happy. If you remember from the very early chapters, your Fashion Persona is a reflection of how you feel on the inside. The inner you is the most authentic you, the real you. When you know and acknowledge your Persona, and when you dress according to the expressions of that Persona, the inner you and the outer you are in harmony. Not only do you look good but you also feel good. No one can take that wonderful feeling of authenticity away from you with a bad look or a weird comment. You have no more discontent with your body size and shape. You have no more "I don't have a thing to wear" days because every piece of clothing and every accessory is something you love. (We realize that this might take

a few shopping trips and maybe months or years, because no one can afford to completely start a wardrobe over—but you are on your way!)

> *"You don't want to be remembered as the sexy one."*
> —JENNIFER LAWRENCE

Of course, every now and then you may begin to doubt yourself, or your confidence may dip. You might worry yourself into a tizzy over what to wear for a big occasion. These are all just temporary situations we all encounter throughout our lives. When they occur, put on a favorite outfit or piece of clothing that makes you feel wonderful. Then remind yourself who you really are. The real you. The beautiful you. Inside and outside.

And now, it's time for you to take the Expressionista Pledge.

On our first page together, we asked you to stand in front of a mirror and describe what you see. Go back to that mirror. This time we want you to stand up and say:

I am beautiful inside and out. I know who I am and I will be true to myself. I am not a follower. I am the leader of my own life.

I embrace my Fashion Persona always.

I respect the Fashion Personas of others.

I am an Expressionista for now and forever.

EXPRESSIONISTA QUOTE:

"Know who you are and who others are. Don't try to change them."

Acknowledgments

What an incredible adventure we had writing this book! It began several years ago when Jackie browsed through her Fashion Group International membership directory and found Pamela's bio and phone number. She dialed. "We haven't met," she said, "but do you want to write a book with me?" And so we did.

Along the way we worked with so many wonderful, remarkable people—mostly women and girls—who helped make this book possible. We owe them our deepest appreciation and gratitude for their encouragement, support, and wisdom. Foremost, we thank our agent, Ronnie Ann Herman, who knew exactly how to guide our fledgling manuscript in the very beginning. And a special mention goes to Jan Spivey Gilchrist, who serendipitously introduced us to Ronnie. We also thank our editorial team: Nicole Geiger and Lindsay Brown at Beyond Words Publishing and our developmental editor, Gretchen Stelter of Cogitate Studios. Our talented illustrator Shannon Laskey throughout these pages has transformed our words with her artistic vision. What a delightful group of gals! You embraced our project with enthusiasm and made it better than we ever imagined.

We also thank everyone who helped us with research and resources. Among them are Chicago Public Schools, Step Up Women's Network, Jodi Norgaard, Jill McMillan, Cathryn Goodman and daughter Clara Haeffner, Kathy Lincoln, Heather Berg Giese, Bonita Chapman, plus all the amazing Expressionistas we met around the country! And then there are those who lovingly cheered us on: Jackie's business support group, Pamela's writing circle, and our wonderful husbands—Richard Dunscomb and Arnold Shifrin. Thank you many times over.

Celebrate yourself!
Jackie and Pamela

Appendix A

THE DOCTOR OF CLOSETOLOGY IS IN

Dear Dr. Jackie: I have many more clothes than a lot of my friends, but I never seem to have anything to wear. What am I doing wrong?

Answer: Even though your closet and dresser are full, it sounds as though you don't have the clothes that fit your personal style. Perhaps you bought things because you were in a hurry or because someone you admire bought them. Now your inner Expressionista looks at them and says, "That's not me!" Take the Fashion Persona Quiz to see who you really are. Any time you buy something new, make sure it matches up with your Persona. Then you'll always have clothes that you like and feel great in!

• •

Dear Dr. Jackie: My mom has so many rules for me. She won't let me wear miniskirts or short shorts. All my friends do. How can I talk her into letting me wear what I want?

Answer: When your mom has a problem with what you are wearing, ask her why. Use a calm voice, not an angry or whiny one. Choose a time when she isn't stressed out from her day. Maybe her reasons are not what you expect. When you hear them, maybe you will agree. Another approach is to see if you can compromise. One mom I know won't allow her Expressionista to leave the house wearing pants with words printed across her derrière. She and her daughter reached a compromise: Her daughter could own a pair, but she agreed to wear them only at home or in the backyard.

• •

Dear Dr. Jackie: There's a designer purse I really want. It's so beautiful! My mom says we can't afford it, and if anyone is going to get one, it's going to be her. How can I get this bag for myself?

Answer: I understand how much you wish to have one of these bags. Most likely there are some girls in your school who already own one. Perhaps you and your mom can visit consignment stores in your area to see if you can find a gently used bag by this designer or maybe the two of you can find one on eBay. If not, would you think about starting a handbag savings account? Deposit any birthday or holiday money, and ask your parents if they will pay you for doing extra chores.

(If they agree, make sure you do a really good job.) You can prove how much this means to you if you can save enough to pay for almost all of this purchase.

• •

Dear Dr. Jackie: My mom still picks out all my clothes. Sometimes she even buys me things when I'm not with her! How can I let her know I am old enough to wear what I want?

Answer: Your mother was your first fashion stylist, and it sounds like she enjoys the role. I imagine it is hard for her to think you might not need her as much anymore. Why not show her the Fashion Persona Quiz and discuss your answers with her? (An adult version can be found in my first book, *I Don't Have a Thing to Wear: The Psychology of Your Closet*.) It can be fun to do the quiz together and see the ways you two are alike and how you are different. Another idea is to cut photos of clothing items you would choose for yourself from catalogs and magazines. With this information, your mom might realize what your tastes really are.

• •

Dear Dr. Jackie: On weekends, I live with my dad, and he buys me clothes. Then I go home, and Mom won't let me wear them. I don't understand.

Answer: What does your mom say about the clothes your dad buys? Does she feel they aren't appropriate for your age? (Be honest—is she right?) Or does she feel bad because she can't afford to buy them for you? Look for the reasons behind her feelings. Maybe she's caught up in her own mixed feelings about the divorce. You might have to wear the clothes just when you're with your dad. I'm sorry you have to deal with this.

• •

Dear Dr. Jackie: I hate my hair. It just hangs there and never looks styled. Do you have any suggestions?

Answer: What is your hair type? That's the first thing to know. Is it naturally straight or curly or somewhere in between? Then you need to find a style that works with that type. You'll always be frustrated if you try to straighten curly tresses (boy, do I ever know this, as you can tell from my tight ringlets!) or keep a curl in straight ones. Don't fight what comes naturally. And stock up on headbands, barrettes, and butterfly clips. Perhaps your mom or dad will treat you to a professional styling before the next big event in your life.

• •

Dear Dr. Jackie: I love my grandma, and she's always shopping for clothes for me. But she likes little bows and bunnies and other cutesy designs. It's just not my style. Is there a way I can get her to change without hurting her feelings?

Answer: I'm thrilled that you have such a warm relationship with your grandmother! Lucky you! And your maturity shows in that you are sensitive to her feelings. Here's what's happening: your grandma sees you as a sweet little girl. She might always feel that way about you. Try spending some time with her going through catalogs or fashion magazines. Show her some pieces you like and tell her why you like them. Perhaps she'll see that your tastes are changing. If not, maybe your mom can put in a good word for you that a red rhinestone hoodie—or whatever you are currently coveting—is at the top of your wish list.

• •

Dear Dr. Jackie: I like to create outfits that are really different, like mixing stripes and metallics and lace all together. My friends sometimes make fun of me, but I like the way I look. I don't want to look like they do. How can I respond to them?

Answer: You have a unique sense of style. Congratulations on being an Expressionista! If you're happy with how you look, that's all that really matters. Explain your Fashion Persona to your friends, and tell them they have Fashion Personas as well. Give them the Fashion Persona Quiz to learn theirs!

• •

Dear Dr. Jackie: My family doesn't have the money for me to dress the way the popular girls do. I'm so embarrassed about it that some days I don't want to go to school. What can I do?

Answer: I understand how you feel but, truly, it doesn't take a lot of money to look sensational. Take the Fashion Persona Quiz to learn your true fashion personality. Find pictures of outfits and individual pieces you like that reflect that personality. You can recreate these looks by shopping in stores that specialize in trendy, low-cost fashion. Some of them even offer designer collections at affordable prices. Resale shops and Goodwill stores often have great selections of not-quite-new and vintage clothing. Find out when they are having sales.

• •

Dear Dr. Jackie: I have to share a room and a closet with my little sister. She steals my stuff and leaves messes all the time. When I want to wear something, I can't find it.

Answer: It's so very hard to share a closet with someone, especially when you have a different way of organizing your clothes. You should be just a little bit flattered—your sister is taking your clothes because she wants to look like you. See if there is a way you can divide the closet with her things on one side and your things on the other. You can put tape on the floor or hang a garment bag to mark the center. Offer to spend time with your sister or to teach her something (like how to make a smooth ponytail)—after she cleans her side of the room.

• •

Dear Dr. Jackie: How old do I have to be to wear shoes with higher heels? Suri Cruise wore kitten heels when she was three. I'm eleven.

Answer: What kind of high heels do you want to wear? It might be appropriate, with parental permission, for girls as young as five or six to wear a small kitten heel. As you get older, you can go for higher heels. Remember that raised heels can be very hard on your legs and feet, so your parents may not want you to wear them for this reason. As an alternative, ballet flats are very popular for all ages. Some styles are extremely dressy if you want to feel more glamorous.

• •

Dear Dr. Jackie: I took the Fashion Persona Quiz, but I still don't know where I fit. Sometimes I feel like a tomboy, but other times I love dresses and little heels. How do I know who I am?

Answer: First of all, don't be alarmed if your quiz answers fall into two or more Persona categories. Very few girls or women are a single Persona at all times. We all have a main Fashion Persona, but we also have touches of the others. For example, I'm a Classic, but I love bold, dramatic jewelry and designer shoes.

Another thing to remember is that you are at an age where you are experimenting with fashion and learning about what you like and don't like. Lucky you—that's what being an Expressionista is about. Take the quiz again every so often, and eventually your dominant Persona will reveal itself.

• •

Dear Dr. Jackie: How can I become a fashion buyer?

Answer: It's obvious you have a love of clothes and style just by asking this question. Keep studying what people wear and why they wear it. When you are of the age to have your first job, you may want to work in stores that sell the types of clothes you enjoy. You'll learn what this career is all about. If you find you want to go farther, there are many good colleges that offer programs in fashion merchandising. Your school's career adviser or an internet search can help you find them. Good luck to you!

• •

Dear Dr. Jackie: How can I become a fashion writer?

Answer: I'm going to let my partner, Pamela, answer this one. She's been writing about fashion for newspapers and magazines for many years. She says: If you have an eye for fashion and you love your English classes, just start writing. Does your school have a newspaper? See if you can contribute articles. That's actually how I got my start. (My very first story was about gray raincoats when I was a junior in high school.) You can also create videos about fashion for your very own YouTube channel or start writing a blog. Good luck to you!

• •

Appendix B

MORE FUN EXPRESSIONISTA QUIZZES

. . . .

QUIZ
What Do Your Nails Say about You?

. . . .

Fashion Personas show up in clothing, accessories, hairstyles, makeup, and even how we groom our fingernails and toenails. Let's test your knowledge. Which Fashion Persona would wear each of the following manicure styles? You might get some ideas for your next manicure or identify the Fashion Personas of people you know. The answers are at the end.

1. I like to put bright decals and jewels on top of my nail polish.

2. My nail treatment is simple: short, filed, and buffed.

3. This week I'm wearing bright orange with white polka dots.

4. My favorite nail polish color is pale pink.

5. I like a french manicure the best.

6. I don't want any polish on my fingernails.

7. Lately I've been wearing pale-blue polish.

8. My toenails and fingernails have to match.

9. I'll wear decals of cartoon characters on my nails.

10. I paint my toenails but not my fingernails.

Answers: 1. Dramatic; 2. Natural; 3. Trend Tracker; 4. Romantic; 5. Classic; 6. Natural; 7. Romantic or Trend Tracker; 8. Classic; 9. Romantic or Dramatic, depending on how bold the decals are; 10. Natural

· ·

QUIZ

Are You Picture Perfect?

· ·

Your photograph reveals much more than what you look like. It also tells how you feel about yourself and how you want others to see you. In fact, you have a Picture Persona just as you have a Fashion Persona. Take this quiz to learn more about yours. Answer each of the following questions with the answer that fits you the best. Most girls find their Picture Persona matches up with their primary or secondary Fashion Personas. You might pick up some new ideas for taking or making some great photographs! Scoring is at the end.

1. Today was school picture day. What did you wear?
   A. My normal school clothes: khakis, T-shirt, and hooded sweatshirt
   B. An outfit I carefully put together last week
   C. Something new I bought just for today
   D. I borrowed my sister's favorite white lace shrug
   E. A bright, beaded necklace and matching hair ornament I made myself

2. How do you feel about vacation photos?
   A. I like unplanned pictures better than posed pictures.
   B. I look for the best location to have my picture taken.
   C. I am always ready to have my picture taken.
   D. I want to change my clothes and brush my hair first.
   E. Great—if I can wear the shorts and top I copied from a fashion magazine.

3. Your favorite photo pose is:
   A. Action
   B. Nice smile
   C. Megawatt smile
   D. With my puppy or American Girl doll
   E. Pose I copied from *America's Next Top Model*

4. When it comes to creating memories, you are usually:
   A. Smiling or laughing
   B. Organizing a group picture with everyone lined up
   C. In every picture
   D. Happy to be in the picture as long as I look good
   E. Planning a fun picture with everyone doing something different

5. Your favorite family photo is:
   A. The one of everyone at the beach
   B. The one from my at-home birthday party
   C. All of them
   D. The one at Disney World with Mickey
   E. The one when we went to New York City

Scoring: Add up the number of As, Bs, and so on. Write your totals down.

If you have mostly As: Your Picture Persona is Natural. You live in the moment, without being self-conscious when the camera shutter clicks.

If you have mostly Bs: Your Picture Persona is Classic. You are a careful and confident planner who uses photography to capture the important events in your life.

If you have mostly Cs: Your Picture Persona is Dramatic. You know how to get yourself noticed by striking the perfect (and maybe a little outrageous) pose.

If you have mostly Ds: Your Picture Persona is Romantic. You want to be dressed up and looking your absolute prettiest before your picture is taken.

If you have mostly Es: Your Picture Persona is Trend Tracker. You need to be in charge of the picture taking, and you know exactly how you want to look!

· ·

QUIZ
What Is Your Bedroom's Fashion Persona?

· ·

Fashion Personas are much more than clothing. They apply to all style choices, including how you decorate your home, the types of gifts you like to give and receive, and the kind of car you will someday drive. This quiz looks at your bedroom—your personal space at home. Your parents may have made the big decisions, like furniture, but you give input and add your own special touches to make the room your own. Even if you share a bedroom with a sibling or two, there are certainly areas or elements that say, "This is me." Answer each question with the response that is most like your bedroom or the bedroom you would like to have. Most girls find their Bedroom Persona matches up with their primary or secondary Fashion Personas. Whether you want to decorate your space to reflect your Persona or try a brand new one, this quiz will give you some great decorating ideas! Scoring is at the end.

1. What color are your bedroom's walls?
   A. Three walls are white and one is dark blue.
   B. Pale pink
   C. White
   D. Apple green
   E. Wallpapered in a star design

2. Describe your sheets and comforter or bedspread:
   A. Cream-colored sheets and a cream-and-navy plaid spread
   B. White sheets, a pink-and-green flowered spread, and a white dust ruffle
   C. White sheets and a white spread
   D. Matching sheets and comforter in green-and-blue stripes
   E. Matching sheets and spread with designer logo on the pillowcases

3. Tell us about your furniture:
   A. Matching pieces in dark wood
   B. White-painted wood with flowery drawer knobs my mom added later
   C. Light wood dresser; no headboard—I just lie on pillows propped up against the wall or on the floor
   D. A big brass bed and white modular furniture with red drawers
   E. A matched set from a children's specialty store that creates dream bedrooms

4. How do you decorate the walls?

A. Photographs of friends and family, bookshelves, and my jewelry hanging on hooks

B. Posters of my favorite princess characters, photos of my friends and pets, and pegs for my hats and headbands

C. A poster of my favorite sports team, bookshelves filled with trophies and team photos

D. Posters of celebrities and bands I love, but I change them a lot; photos of me in school plays; one wall has a full-length mirror

E. A big bulletin board so I can pin up pictures of runway outfits I like, photos of me dressed up for special occasions

5. What else is in your bedroom?

A. A couple of accent pillows that match my bedspread, a computer desk, and study lamp

B. Lots of stuffed animals and dolls, a collection of vacation souvenirs, scrapbooks

C. A small chest at the end of my bed for athletic equipment, my shell collection

D. Baskets to hold all my accessories, a mirrored vanity table

E. A magazine rack, art books, bins for my craft and sewing projects

Scoring: Add up how many of each response you have. Write your totals down.

If you have mostly As: Your Bedroom Persona is Classic. You like your space to be neat and organized, without a lot of frill.

If you have mostly Bs: Your Bedroom Persona is Romantic. Your space is girly, fun, and cute.

If you have mostly Cs: Your Bedroom Persona is Natural. Your bedroom is plain and simple, and it works for you.

If you have mostly Ds: Your Bedroom Persona is Dramatic. Your surroundings are as bold and bright as you are.

If you have mostly Es: Your Bedroom Persona is Trend Tracker. You frequently make changes and update your personal space.

Appendix C

RESOURCES

READING

I Don't Have a Thing to Wear: The Psychology of Your Closet by Jackie Walker and Judie Taggart is the Doctor of Closetology's first book describing how to use clothing to enhance your self-esteem. It was written for adults, but Expressionistas find it is an easy, enlightening read with even more real-life stories and quizzes to explore (Pocket Books, 2003).

True You: A Journey to Finding and Loving Yourself by Janet Jackson and David Ritz tells about actress and singer Janet Jackson and her personal struggles to overcome her low self-esteem (Simon & Schuster, 2011).

Saranormal is a book series about the adventures of Sara Collins, a twelve-year-old who can see ghosts and communicate with spirits (saranormalbooks.com; Simon & Schuster).

The Best Friend Thief by Laurel-Ann Dooley explores the complexities of best-friend relationships (WordWorks Publishing, 2011).

Girls' Life Magazine is a bimonthly chock-full of information and advice about every aspect of daily living: relationships, current events, fashion, school, and more (girlslife.com).

Discovery Girls is a bimonthly magazine created by girls for girls. Articles cover school, clothes, friendships, family, and problem solving and include quizzes and craft instructions (discoverygirls .com/magazine).

ORGANIZATIONS, CAMPAIGNS, AND WEBSITES

Girls on the Run International encourages and inspires girls in the third through the eighth grades to be joyful, healthy, and confident through running. The program has two components: a fun, hands-on curriculum that focuses on self-discovery, and uplifting workouts. The culmination of each twelve-week season is a noncompetitive 5K running event. For more information: girlsontherun.org

The Bully Project is a crusade to stop children from being bullied by their peers. *Bully*, the 2012 documentary by Lee Hirsch and the Weinstein Company, follows several families who have been affected by bullying. The website, thebullyproject.com, includes personal stories and inspiration. The online Toolkit for Students teaches how to stand up to bullies, how to stop bullying in your community, and safe internet strategies.

The It Gets Better Project, founded by Dan Savage and Terry Miller, gives hope, encouragement, and support to lesbian, gay, bisexual, and transgendered youth who may be bullied and harassed for being different. Find inspirational videos and camaraderie on the website itgetsbetter.org. Or read *It Gets Better: Coming Out, Overcoming Bullying, and Creating a Life Worth Living* by Dan Savage and Terry Miller (Dutton, 2011).

Dove Self-Esteem Toolkit and Resources: dove.us/Social-Mission/Self-Esteem-Toolkit-And-Resources/default.aspx

Youngzine is a news and current-events website designed for young students who are curious about the world. They can win points and badges for reviewing stories and submitting articles to the U Write section (youngzine.com).

Rookie is an online magazine for girls founded by teen fashion blogger Tavi Gevinson. Updated daily, the site includes sections on lifestyle, music, media, how-to, and fiction (rookiemag.com).

Hello Giggles is an interactive entertainment website for smart, creative girls and women founded by actress and musician Zooey Deschanel. You can contribute—send your favorite photos and videos to hellogiggles.com.

The Born This Way Foundation was founded by Lady Gaga and her mother, Cynthia Germanotta, to create a braver, kinder world society where differences and individuality are accepted and celebrated (bornthiswayfoundation.org).

Educating Jane is a website for girls, parents, and educators dedicated to helping girls grow with self-esteem, self-awareness, and involvement in the world. The girls-only section includes leadership advice, career exploration, body weight and healthy eating guides, and money management (educatingjane.com).

YouTube's Hello Style channel is a video library of advice and how-to videos from your favorite fashion magazines. Topics include how to create runway looks, how to go vintage shopping, fashion don'ts, sample workouts, penny-pinching beauty, plus-size dressing, and much more (youtube.com/hellostyle).

YouTube's Seven Cool Tweens channel shows high-energy tweens as they model their favorite outfits, explain their beauty routines, make dresses from garbage bags, and offer insight into their life-style. The parent-controlled site is at youtube.com/sevencooltweens.

The Pink Locker Society is a girls-only book series about middle school life and PBBs (periods, bras, and boys). The companion website, pinklockersociety.org, includes sample chapters, recipes, and craft projects. Get your questions answered or give your best advice on the PLS blog.

Daughters.com is an online and print magazine by New Moon Girls. Topics covered include relationships, family life, communication, health, and education. Sign up for a free e-newsletter.

Powered by Girl is a girl-driven activist website that exposes negative gender stereotypes in popular culture media and promotes positive messaging (poweredbygirl.org).

Girls Inc. inspires girls to be strong, smart, and bold through educational programs and activities. Girls ages six through eighteen can participate in local groups and online (girlsinc.org).

About-Face is a website that teaches girls and women to understand and resist harmful media messages that affect self-esteem and body image (about-face.org).

ENTERTAINMENT

Bully, a 2011 documentary, exposes the widespread problem of bullying through the heartbreaking stories of five children who are bullied by their classmates. It also shows how their torment affects families, schools, and communities and how clueless some adults can be. Distributed by the Weinstein Company.

Wicked: The Untold Story of the Witches of Oz is a warm-hearted musical that shows how two very different witches create a unique friendship. One is a Romantic and the other is Naturally green.

Pinkalicious the Musical tells the tale of a young girl whose love of the color pink becomes a problem after eating too many pink cupcakes—she turns pink! Eventually she learns it's best to always be yourself.

Bullied to Silence is a 2012 documentary that features the stories of bullies and dozens of children who have been bullied and offers tools to stop verbal bullying and cyber bullying. Produced by Dog Eats Hat Productions/Purple People Inc. Learn more at bulliedtosilence.com.

SHOPPING AND MORE

How many socks make a pair? At Little MissMatched, a pair is three. Choose your motif, and you'll get three different socks in similar color and design. No matchy-matchy here, but any two socks you wear will coordinate. The company also sells accessories, apparel, bedding, and dolls, all in zany patterns and bright hues. You'll find them in retail stores and online at littlemismatched.com.

Go! Go! Sports Girls is a collection of cuddly sports-themed dolls, each with a story and advice for healthy living. A secret inspirational message is hidden in each doll's tummy. They are in retail stores and online at gogosportsgirls.com.

Express your Fashion Persona by decorating your school locker. Locker Lookz offers an assortment of color-coordinated wallpaper, rugs, and mirrors—even light-up chandeliers. They are in retail stores or online at lockerlookz.com.

The Mini Social is a (free) membership website that sells hip designer clothing and accessories for moms, babies, and children at prices up to 70 percent off retail. Shop quickly, because many of the sales are for only seventy-two hours (theminisocial.com).

Isabee Tweens is an online specialty boutique of apparel and accessories for fashion-savvy tweens sizes 7–16 (isabeetweens.com).

Izzy and Ash offers fashion-forward designer apparel and accessories for girls ages seven to fourteen (izzyandash.com).

Polyvore is an internet fashion community where you can read industry news, follow bloggers, create collages of products you like from online stores, and buy (polyvore.com).